THE STORY OF THE WORLD

BOOK V.

THE GROWTH OF THE BRITISH EMPIRE

FROM WATERLOO TO THE PRESENT DAY
1815-1903

OFF TO THE COLONIES

THE GROWTH OF THE BRITISH EMPIRE

BY

M. B. SYNGE

ILLUSTRATED BY E. M. SYNGE, A.R.E.

YESTERDAY'S CLASSICS

CHAPEL HILL, NORTH CAROLINA

This edition, first published in 2006 by Yesterday's Classics, is an unabridged republication of the work originally published by William Blackwood and Sons in 1904. For a full listing of books published by Yesterday's Classics, visit www.yesterdaysclassics.com. Yesterday's Classics is the publishing arm of the Baldwin Project which presents the complete text of dozens of classic books for children at www.mainlesson.com under the editorship of Lisa M. Ripperton and T. A. Roth.

ISBN-10:   1-59915-017-4
ISBN-13:   978-1-59915-017-8

Yesterday's Classics
PO Box 3418
Chapel Hill, NC 27515

CONTENTS

CHAPTER 1

HOW SPAIN LOST SOUTH AMERICA

"So grew and gathered through the silent years
The madness of a people, wrong by wrong."
—LOWELL.

THE storms of war had passed away and Europe was at peace. But, like the waves after a great storm, the influences that had worked for freedom, continued to work. For two centuries, this sixth part of the world, had been governed by Spaniards and Portuguese: for two centuries, she had borne the oppression of despotic viceroys sent from Spain, whose cruelties defy description. It was small wonder then that, with the spirit of revolution in the air, the people of South America should rise and fight to free themselves from Spain.

Brazil belonged to Portugal, and the hatred of the people towards the Portuguese, not being so bitter, the country worked out its freedom by more peaceful means. The Spanish colonies rose after the deposition of their king by Napoleon.

It is impossible to follow the many battles that took place during the next twelve years: let us rather tell the story of two heroes, whose names stand out clearly against the horizon of South American history, as the liberators of their country—Bolivar and San Martin.

The earliest plans for the revolution, that was to free South America from the yoke of Spain, were laid by a secret society in London, founded by Miranda. England herself took no part; but Bolivar and San Martin both caught the enthusiasm of the master, and swore to do all in their power to carry out Miranda's ideas. Both men sailed for South America.

San Martin landed at Buenos Ayres in the year 1812—an unknown man. He at once roused the people of Argentina, a country ten times the size of Great Britain and Ireland, called from the great silver river—La Plata, which flowed through it. It is one of the richest territories in the world to-day, and largely populated by European emigrants. San Martin, who had served in Spanish armies for twenty years, soon fired the enthusiasm of the people. An army was raised, which soon became famous under his leadership. It was not long before the arms of Spain were torn down, to be replaced by the blue and white colours of the revolutionists, the cruel tortures of the Spanish Inquisition were abolished, and the last links with the mother country broken. Early in the year 1816—the year after Waterloo—Argentina declared her independence.

The spirit of revolution had meanwhile spread to the neighbouring province of Chili, a strip of country between the high Andes and the Pacific Ocean, so called from the Peruvian word for snow. But the Spaniards were strong in Peru, and marching south, they defeated the Chilians, under the leadership of the famous Irishman O'Higgins. He now looked to San Martin for help. But the mighty range of the Andes, rising between the two provinces, was considered quite impassable. Nevertheless San Martin determined to march to the aid of Chili. And the march of the army of the Andes is one of the most brilliant feats ever recorded in the world's military history. It is a feat that ranks with Hannibal's famous passage over the snowy Alps and Napoleon's march to Marengo.

Having set themselves free, this army of patriots was ready to face the colossal task, of helping their brothers across the Andes to free themselves. Everything was prepared at Mendoza, at the western feet of the mountains. Here an arsenal was established, where cannon, shot, and shell were cast, church bells were melted down, and forges blazed by day and night. The patriotic women of Mendoza made blue cloth for the uniforms, and early in January 1817, all was ready for the start. There was high holiday in the town; the streets were decked with flags, and the army marched forth to receive its flag, embroidered by the women of the city.

"Soldiers!" cried San Martin, waving the flag above his head, "this is the first independent flag,

3

which has been blessed in America. Swear to sustain it and to die in defence of it—as I swear I do."

"We swear!" rose from four thousand throats.

Off started the army under the guidance of San Martin and O'Higgins. It would take too long to tell of the bitter days and nights, endured by these brave soldiers of Argentina, as they struggled over the snow-clad passes. Ridge after ridge rose before them, terrible with ice and snow, treacherous with chasms and precipices. Mules, horses, and men dropped dead in the icy winds, that swept down from the lofty summits. But their noble efforts were crowned with success. Three weeks from the start, the army of the Andes descended on the plains of Chili, surprised and defeated the Spanish army, and marched triumphantly into Santiago, the capital. Chilian independence was won, and O'Higgins was made the first governor of the new republic.

Much had been done. Spanish rule had been checked, but not yet broken. Its grip was still on Peru, and her people were crying aloud for freedom, like their neighbours. The way to Peru from Chili lay by sea, and the Spanish fleet lay off Callao, the port of Lima. It was at this moment, that the famous British sailor Lord Cochrane came upon the scene. One November day in 1818, he landed at Valparaiso, the port of Chili, ready to place his services at the disposal of the revolutionists.

Though broken on land, the Spanish shore was not conquered. Peru still lay in the hands of the oppressor, and the Spanish fleet in its harbours was ready to sail south to attack the Chilians, when Lord Cochrane, trained in the school of Nelson, appeared on the scene. He was given command of the Chilian fleet, and soon swept the Spaniards from the sea.

Having thus made Chili mistress of her own waters, it was possible to begin the liberation of Peru.

CHAPTER 2

THE HEROES OF INDEPENDENCE

"The time is ripe, is rotten-ripe, for change,
Then let it come."
—LOWELL.

WHILE San Martin, O'Higgins, and Cochrane were working to free the southern provinces of South America from the yoke of Spain, Bolivar was at work with the master-spirit, Miranda, in the north.

When little more than a boy, young Bolivar had stood with his tutor amid the ruins of Rome— the city of the Cæsars. In a moment of enthusiasm, he had seized his tutor's hands and sworn to liberate his native land. Did the dream of his life also come to him here,—that of ruling over a united South American republic? He went to London, became an enthusiastic disciple of Miranda, renewed the oath made on the sacred hill of Rome, and returned to South America with Miranda to fulfil his promise.

So successful were the liberators, that in the summer of 1811, Venezuela was ready to declare her independence, as the first republic in South America.

All was going well, when the terrible earthquake of 1812 devastated the capital, Caracas. For many weeks, not a single drop of rain had fallen, and a day had been set apart for all the people to pray in the churches, as with one voice, for the much-needed rain. The sky was cloudless, the heat intense. It was four o'clock in the afternoon—the churches were crowded. Suddenly a tremendous roar was heard from the neighbouring hills, the ground rocked violently to and fro, and in a few minutes five large towns, including Caracas, were in ruins, under which lay buried some 20,000 people.

The first republic of Venezuela had found its grave. Panic spread among the revolutionists. Miranda, loaded with chains, was sent to Spain, to languish in a dungeon at Cadiz till he died. Bolivar had to flee. But he was undaunted. He determined to reconquer Venezuela. He collected an army, and in a short time gained for himself a place, among the most famous leaders of his time. With 600 men, in ninety days, he fought six battles; he defeated 4500 men, captured fifty Spanish guns, and restored the republic in Venezuela.

He entered Caracas in triumph, amid the ringing of bells and the roar of cannon. People shouted for their "Liberator"; his path was strewn with flowers; beautiful maidens in white led his horse, and decked his brow with a laurel crown. And Bolivar delighted in this display. There was nothing very heroic in his appearance at this time. Short and rugged, with an olive skin and black deep-set eyes, he wore his black curling hair tied behind, after the fashion of the age. Such was the Dictator of Venezuela in 1813.

But fortune now deserted the revolutionists. The Spaniards collected in force and defeated them. Bolivar was obliged to flee to Jamaica. He spent his exile planning a new war of independence. One night, he narrowly escaped death. The Spaniards had hired a man to kill him, and it was only owing to the fact that his secretary was sleeping in his hammock, that the secretary was slain and not Bolivar.

A few years later, he landed once more in South America to renew the struggle. In none of the colonies was fighting so stubborn, so heroic, so full of tragedy, as in Venezuela. Twice conquered, she rose a third time against her oppressors, ever encouraged by Bolivar. For a time, the Liberator was met by nothing but defeat. His courage was magnificent.

"The day of America has come!" he cried. "Before the sun has again run his annual course, Liberty will have dawned throughout your land."

The next step was perhaps his greatest. He crossed the Andes and captured the capital of New Granada, changing the whole aspect of affairs at one supreme stroke. It was even a more wonderful feat than that of San Martin. It was June 1819. To tell the story of his passage would be but to repeat that of San Martin. There was the same intense cold, the same awful dangers to be faced, but without the careful preparation made at Mendoza. The men under Bolivar were ill-clad, and over one hundred died, while struggling manfully over the snow-covered summits of the Andes. It was a mere skeleton army that descended from the heights into the beautiful valley, where lay the capital of New Granada. The Spaniards were completely taken by surprise and defeated. And Bolivar marched triumphantly into the city, crowned with laurels. The dream of his life was now accomplished. Venezuela and New Granada were thrown into a huge province called Columbia, under the presidency of Bolivar. To the Columbians he cried in his joy: "From the banks of the Orinoco to the Andes of Peru, the liberating army, marching from one triumph to another, has covered with its protecting arms the whole of Columbia."

Soon he had annexed the neighbouring province, whose capital was Quito.

Both San Martin and Bolivar were now advancing on Peru, "the last battlefield in America," as Bolivar said. The moment had come, when the two liberators must meet, to discuss the future of the revolution. San Martin hoped they would be able to work together for the good of their country. But their aims were different. San Martin had no personal ambition: he only wished to see South America freed from the yoke of Spain. Bolivar wished to be President of a united country, and that country one of the largest in the world. The two men met. It was July 1822. They embraced one another warmly, and held a long private interview. It was followed by a banquet and a ball. Bolivar proposed the first toast: "To the two greatest men of South America—General San Martin and myself."

The ball followed. In the middle of it San Martin crept away. He had seen clearly that he and Bolivar could never act together. In a spirit of generosity, unsurpassed in history, he left to Bolivar the completion of his life's work. To him should be "the glory of finishing the war for the independence of South America."

"There is no room in Peru for both Bolivar and myself," he said afterwards to his faithful friend Guido. "He will come to Peru. Let him come, so that America may triumph."

Then he embraced Guido and rode away into the darkness, never to return. He died in voluntary exile in 1850.

The coast was now clear, and Bolivar soon became absolute master of Peru. He thought that all America was his. With the splendid forces of the Argentina army left him by San Martin, he passed from strength to strength. A new Republic was named after him—Bolivia. But his supreme power in 1828 roused the suspicions of the people. They dreaded a second Cæsar—a second Napoleon. A conspiracy to slay him failed, but it forced Bolivar to resign. He died in exile in 1830.

Such is the story of the two men who helped to free South America from Spain. Statues at Caracas and Lima were raised to commemorate the splendid work of Bolivar, but the work of the man, who was ready to sacrifice all, for the good of his country, needs no monuments—for history does not forget such as these.

CHAPTER 3

THE GREEK WAR

"Hellenes of past ages,
 Oh, start again to life!
 At the sound of my trumpet breaking
 Your sleep! Oh, join with me
 And the seven-hilled city seeking
 Fight, conquer, till we're free!"
                —*Riga's War-song.*

BEFORE ever South America had won her independence, another country had felt the tyranny of oppression, and had already begun to struggle into the fuller air of freedom. That country was Greece—the land of Homer and Socrates—the land of Marathon and Thermopylæ. Greece had been subject to Rome, till Constantine built a new Rome and Constantinople became the capital of the Eastern Empire. Under this Byzantine Empire, Greece had remained, till the capture of Constantinople by the Turks in 1453. Under Turkish rule the Greeks had suffered deeply, and that nation, once so famous in Europe, now lay paralysed under its Mohammedan oppressors.

THE GREEK WAR

When the Greek revolution began, in 1821, it was no sudden insurrection to which the people were stung. As a tree, which winter has stripped of its leaves, puts forth fresh growth in the spring, so the time had come, when the long winter of Turkish oppression must pass and spring must dawn. The War of Independence in North and South America, and the outburst of suppressed France, gave the Greeks courage to arise and assert their newly recognised strength.

In the opening scenes of the insurrection, the barbarity of Greek and Turks was perhaps on a level. The Greeks revenged themselves as fiercely as a slave, who had broken his fetters: the Turks resorted to wholesale massacre. Europe could not watch a struggle, so heroic, so prolonged, so full of tragedy, without being strangely moved. British volunteers, among them Lord Cochrane of Chilian fame, and Byron the poet, lent their services to the cause of Greek freedom. Byron still dreamt of a Greece, on whose free soil the arts and sciences should once more flourish in their ancient glory. At the moment of his arrival, in 1823, Greece was split up into parties. She had no leader, and things were going badly for her. Mesolonghi, one of the strongholds of western Greece, was besieged by the Turks. They stood at the entrance of the Gulf of Patras, in a plain stretching away from the sea-coast to the mountains. Much of the country was little better than a swamp, inhabited by fishermen. Byron's arrival here was hailed with enthusiasm. Crowds of citizens gathered on the beach to receive him, and shouts arose as he stepped ashore in a scarlet uniform. It was January 1824. His very presence gave them encouragement. His interest in them was very real, and it is likely he would have done much. But Mesolonghi was a bed of fever, and four months after his arrival, Byron died in the midst of the Greeks he had come to serve.

"I have given Greece my time, my means, my health; and now I give her my life!" he cried almost with his dying breath.

Perhaps his death—in the glorious attempt to restore Greece to her ancient freedom and renown—served Greece better than his life could ever have done. All the Greek patriotism seemed now to be corked up within the walls of Mesolonghi, where an undisciplined population did the duty of a trained garrison, and warm-hearted peasants the work of a trained army. The Turkish commander had invested the city by land and sea, but the Greek garrison had a good supply of food within, and moreover a Greek fleet was known to be on its way with supplies. One July morning at early dawn the Greeks saw the distant sea covered with vessels. Their joy was boundless. It was their fleet, and it would enable them to defeat the Turks. But suddenly the red flag of Turkey became visible to their straining eyes, and they discovered it was thirty-nine ships of war to block their port, and no Greek ships. Soon after this, came six Turkish chiefs to offer terms. The Greeks were indignant. With one voice they cried, in a spirit worthy of the Spartans of old, "War!"

The summer passed. Famine threatened the city. A few old Greek chiefs were in favour of treating.

"What, old men," cried the garrison, "do you hold life so dear at your age, when we, in the flower of youth, would give it up? If the men of Mesolonghi cannot defend their walls, they will defend their liberty. There shall be no capitulation as long as one of us remains alive. The Turkish standard shall not fly in Mesolonghi, till it has been carried over our dead bodies."

Still the Greek fleet did not come. It alone could save the brave defenders.

Meanwhile the Sultan of Turkey grew furious with his commander. "I will have Mesolonghi or your head," he cried.

The tardy arrival of the Greek fleet brought joy to the defenders, and alarm spread through the ranks of the Turks. The Sultan now called in the Egyptian army under Ibraham. The Egyptians came on, boasting that they would make short work of Mesolonghi, but when they met the Greeks hand-to-hand, they were thoroughly defeated.

Still the spirit of Greek heroism, rare in the Greek revolution, rare even in the history of mankind, kept the flag flying over Mesolonghi.

Then Ibraham ordered a fleet of flat-bottomed boats to be built, and launched upon the lagoons between the city and the open sea. Mesolonghi was thus completely surrounded.

The siege had lasted a year. The food was exhausted, the last charge of powder had been fired, when the Greeks—men, women, and children—joined in one last reckless, heroic assault, and perished, fighting their way through the Turkish lines.

Their splendid defence had achieved its end. The powers of Europe could no longer hold aloof. England, France, and Russia agreed to send help. In 1827 a combined fleet under an English sailor, Sir Edward Codrington, appeared in Greek waters. Codrington was one of Nelson's school, and had commanded a ship at the battle of Trafalgar.

The combined fleets of Turkey and Egypt—a great armament of sixty-five sail—lay in the Bay of Navarino. They formed a huge crescent in the mouth of the bay, with fire-ships at either end. On the afternoon of October 20, the English Admiral, on board a stately wooden three-decker, sailed into the bay. He was followed by the French and Russians. He did not mean to fight. But suddenly one of the fire-ships discharged a volley into an English ship, whose commander fired back. Soon a deep roar resounded through the crescent. The battle of Navarino had begun. For four hours it raged. Codrington poured a very tempest of fire into the Turkish flag-ship, until she drifted away, a total wreck, having lost 650 men out of a crew of 850. Then he turned to the Egyptian flag-ship, and ten minutes later she too was a wreck. When evening fell, most of the Turkish and Egyptian ships were in flames. All through the night, the hills round

Navarino shone with the light of burning ships. When morning dawned, what remained of the crescent of ships had vanished.

The allied fleets had saved Greece. It was some years yet, before Greece finally won her independence. There was more fighting to be done by land and sea. But at last in the year 1833, young Otho of Bavaria landed in Greece, to be crowned amid the shouts of the people, as their first King.

CHAPTER 4

VICTORIA—QUEEN OF ENGLAND

"Far away beyond her myriad coming changes earth will be
Something other than the wildest modern guess of you or me."
—TENNYSON.

GREECE had fought for and won her independence, and the Bavarian boy-king Otho, had reigned for four years, when an event of great importance took place in England.

After a short reign, King William IV. died in 1837, leaving his niece, the Princess Victoria, heir to the throne. The Princess was but eighteen. She had been carefully trained by her widowed mother for the great position she would one day fill. She was taught to be "self-reliant, brave, and systematical." She learnt prudence and economy, as though she were born to be poor. The story of her accession is well known, but it must be told yet again. It was early in the morning hours of June 20, when the old king died at Windsor, and messengers were soon hurrying off to Kensington Palace in London to carry the tidings to the young princess. They reached the palace about five o'clock in the morning. All was still within. "They knocked, they rang, they thumped for a considerable time, before they could arouse the porter at the gate. They were again kept waiting in the courtyard, then turned into one of the lower rooms, where they seemed forgotten by everybody. They rang the bell and desired that the attendant of the Princess Victoria might be sent to inform her Royal Highness, that they requested an audience on business of importance. After another delay, and another ringing to inquire the cause, the attendant was summoned, who stated that the princess was in such a sweet sleep, that she could not venture to disturb her."

"But we are come on business of state to the queen, and even her sleep must give way to that," they said.

And a few moments later, the new queen entered the room in a "loose white nightgown and shawl, her nightcap thrown off and her hair falling upon her shoulders, her feet in slippers, tears in her eyes, but perfectly collected and dignified."

So the Princess Victoria became Queen of England, and a new era opened for her country.

The opening of the new reign found some of the greatest discoveries and inventions, which make for civilisation, forcing their way into daily use. Time had dispelled the vague fears of travelling by trains at a speed of over five miles an hour. Stephenson had run the first passenger train in the north of England in 1825. It had reached the alarming speed of twelve miles an hour! Not only was it the first passenger train in England; it was the first in the world. Stephenson was the pioneer. He lightly over-rode all objections.

"Suppose now," said a member of Parliament to him one day—"Suppose now one of your engines, to be going at a speed of ten miles an hour along the railroad, and that a cow were to stray upon the line and get in the way of the engine, would not that be very awkward?"

"Yes," answered the great engineer, with a twinkle in his eye, "very awkward—for the coo."

The year after the queen's accession, railways were opened all over the country, and it was noted as a triumph of human energy and skill, over time and space, that an engine had travelled at the speed of twenty-seven miles an hour. Since the year 1819, when the first historic steamer, the Savannah, had made its way across the Atlantic, from New York to Liverpool in four weeks, more and more sailing ships had been fitted with steam-engines. The year after the queen's accession, the famous Great Western crossed the ocean from Bristol to New York in fifteen days. Regular service was now established with the New World, and Liverpool rose year by year in importance, till she became one of the greatest ports, not only in England, but in Europe.

Yet another means of bridging over time and space, was now established in England, to spread later over the whole world. Up to this time, letter writing had been the luxury of the rich, the cost of postage being too much for poor people to afford. This story is always told concerning the origin of the penny post in England. Coleridge, the English poet, was one day walking through the Lake district in the north, when he saw the postman deliver a letter to a poor woman at her cottage door. The woman turned it over and examined it, and then returned it, saying she could not afford to pay the postage, which was one shilling. Hearing that the letter was from her brother, Coleridge insisted on paying the postage, in spite of evident unwillingness on the part of the woman. As soon as the postman had ridden off, she showed Coleridge how his money had been wasted. The sheet inside the envelope was blank. They had agreed together, that as long as all went well with him, he should send a blank sheet once a quarter, and thus she had tidings without the expense of postage.

Coleridge told this story to an official in the Post Office, named Rowland Hill. It struck him at once that something must be wrong in a system, which drove a brother and sister to cheat, in order to hear of one another. He at once worked out a scheme of reform. London had had a penny post for years. Could this be extended to the country? Rowland Hill was laughed at. "Of all the wild and extravagant schemes I have ever heard of, this is the wildest and most extravagant," cried the Postmaster-General, while others denounced the idea as "nonsense."

Rowland Hill fought on, and at last made things possible by the introduction of a cheap stamp, since adopted throughout the civilised world. To him also thanks are due, for the introduction of the book-post and money orders, none of which were possible, till after the queen's accession.

Another and yet faster means of communication was now burst upon the astonished world. This was the electric telegraph, first opened for use in 1842. The word telegraph explains itself (*tele*, far off, and *grapho*, I write). It was the result of long years of patient toil. But by a curious coincidence, an American and an Englishman in the same year discovered, how the electric current could be brought into practical use for "sounding alarms in distant places."

Thus the very year of the queen's accession, a line of telegraph was constructed on a railway in the north of England, for the use of railway signals; and a little later, it was taught to print the messages it carried, as it does to-day.

Thus science and speed played their great part in the history of England and in the history of the world. Men and countries were no longer cut off from one another. Knowledge grew from more to more; commerce increased by leaps and bounds; colonies grew nearer to the mother country, for the long sea-passage was robbed of half its terrors.

"Not in vain the distance beacons.
    Forward, forward let us range,

Let the great world spin for ever
    down the ringing grooves of change."

CHAPTER 5

THE GREAT BOER TREK

"Come, my friends,
'Tis not too late to seek a newer world."
—TENNYSON.

IT was therefore no small event in the world's history, when in 1826, the first steamer—suitably named the Enterprise—made its way, in two months, from England to the Cape of Good Hope. Let us see how the Cape Colony was getting on. After the battle of Waterloo and the fall of Napoleon, there had been great distress throughout the British Isles, and 5000 emigrants had been sent out to the Cape. These had mostly landed on the sandy beach of Algoa Bay. They settled in a district known as Albany, west of the Great Fish River, and were soon building the now flourishing towns of Port Elizabeth and Grahamstown.

Meanwhile the fair prospects, with which the colony had started in 1807, were clouding over. The colonists, especially the Dutch farmers, were discontented. They refused to conform to the new order of things.

"The English want us to use their ploughs, instead of our old wooden ones," they complained. "But we like our old things best. What satisfied our forefathers can satisfy us."

It was a natural cry, wrung from a people, who had so long been cut off from European intercourse.

Up to this time, the colonists had used the black Hottentots of the country, as well as the negro slaves imported before 1806, to do their work. It had been slowly dawning on the people in Europe, that the position of these Hottentots was very wretched. They were, in fact, no better than the four-legged cattle, that made up the live stock of the colony. They were slaves. In 1833, a bill was passed in England freeing all slaves in the British dominions, and decreeing that they should have equal rights with the white men of the colonies. Now in Cape Colony, there were no less than 39,000 slaves.

Compensation for the loss of their slaves was given to the slave-holders, but it was quite inadequate, and numbers of farmers were utterly ruined. Sir Benjamin D'Urban was now sent out from England to govern Cape Colony, to enforce the new Slave Act and to put Europeans and natives on a better footing. It was his first Christmas at the Cape: on New Year's Eve he had a large party of colonists at the Castle, to welcome in the New Year of 1835. Great good humour prevailed, and no one observed that several times during the evening, the Governor left the merry party, which broke up after midnight. Next morning bad news spread. A large force of Kaffirs had invaded the then frontiers of Cape Colony on Christmas Day; they had burnt every farm, killed the colonists, and carried off their sheep and cattle. The Governor knew the worst on the evening of the party: he had not wished to throw a gloom over the colonists, but he had secretly despatched a force under Sir Harry Smith, in the middle of the night. Five days later, the force reached Grahamstown, to find a state of indescribable panic: 456 farms had been destroyed, 50 Europeans slain. It took a year's fighting to drive the Kaffirs back into their own country.

The Dutch farmers were now thoroughly dissatisfied. They did not approve of much that had been done and left undone, so they determined to take an important step.

South Africa was large. There were vast tracts of country yet unexplored. To the north and east lay a great wild land, where they might live that solitary, wandering, unrestrained life, that had become necessary to them. There they might do as they pleased, vexed by no changes in the laws, burdened by no taxes, worried by no English-speaking people. They would leave their farms in the Cape Colony and wander forth into the wilderness. They likened themselves to the Children of Israel, when they went forth from Egypt, from the oppression of Pharaoh. They knew no history or geography, save that contained in their Bibles, and some, amongst them, had dreamy ideas, that they might reach Jerusalem or the Promised Land.

The region toward which they now set their faces, was only known to European travellers seeking sport and adventure. It was a hunter's paradise. Giraffes, elephants, lions filled the forests and covered the plains; there were hippopotami and rhinoceri abounding in the rivers and swamps.

"It is like a zoological gardens turned out to graze," said an early traveller.

The land itself was brown and arid except during the summer rains, and the Boer farmers found a very wilderness before them, as they made their way into the unknown land. Each householder took his wife and children, his flocks and herds, travelling in large canvas-covered waggons drawn by some 16 oxen. Among these was little Paul Kruger, who at the age of nine followed his father's cattle over stretches of plain and veld. It would take too long to tell the romantic story of their wanderings, their conflicts with the natives, their hardships, their sufferings. Heroically they pushed on to Thaba 'Nchu, near the present town of Bloemfontein in the Orange River Colony. A party, under the leadership of Hendrik Potgieter was the first to arrive. Leaving there a little encampment, Potgieter and eleven comrades went off to explore the country to the north. They returned to find that a number of their party had been massacred, by a band of native warriors, known as the Matabili. There was no time to be lost. Potgieter selected a suitable hill near by, lashed fifty waggons together, filled the open spaces with thorn trees, and with forty brave settlers awaited attack. They had not long to wait. The Matabili rushed upon the laager with loud hisses, to be received by a deadly fire from the defenders. Again and again they rushed on, regardless of death, and with loud war-whoops tried to tear the waggons apart; but the Dutch defended themselves by keeping up a rapid fire, the women loading spare guns for their use, until at last the Matabili had to flee. But they had carried off the emigrants' cattle and left them in great distress. Fortunately a fresh band of emigrants had just arrived under the leadership of Gerrit Maritz, and the two leaders determined to attack the Matabili chief in his kraal.

One hundred and seven farmers mustered for the purpose. At break of day one morning, they surprised the Matabili warriors, who took to flight, only to be hunted by the Dutch farmers, till the sun was high in the heavens and 400 of them lay dead. Then the colonists burnt the kraal and returned in triumph to Thaba 'Nchu with 7000 cattle. They formed a camp near the Vet river and called it Winburg, in memory of their victory. Fresh bands of emigrants were now constantly arriving to take possession of this new land to the south of the river Vaal, north of the Orange river, known to-day as the Orange River Colony.

One specially large party arrived under the leadership of Pieter Retief, whose tragic fate must now be told in the story of Natal.

CHAPTER 6

THE STORY OF NATAL

"Snatched and bartered oft from hand to hand."
—KIPLING.

"IN all the world there is not a fairer country than the pleasant land of Natal." It rises, in terraces, from the shores of the Indian Ocean to the heights of the Drakensberg. It is well watered by numerous streams, the soil is rich, and the climate healthy for Europeans. Some four hundred years before this time, the coast had been discovered by Vasco da Gama one Christmas Day, and this being the natal day of our Lord, he had called it Natal. It was inhabited entirely by natives. Now the solitary passes of the Drakensberg were speckled with the waggons of the hardy Dutch pioneers, who drove their flocks and herds into the green valleys of Natal. The story of their reception by the natives is not pleasant reading.

In the year 1783, a little brown baby had been born on the banks of the Umvolisi River. Chaka, for that was the name of this future Zulu chieftain, grew to manhood with a nature as cruel as Nero, ambitious as Napoleon. He had heard of Napoleon's conquests in Europe, and he now began a career of conquest, until he had made himself chief from the Limpopo or Crocodile river to the southern borders of Natal. Every tribe in his way, he exterminated. He devastated thousands of miles of country, and caused the death of one million human beings. At last he was slain by his brother Dingan, who made himself king over this now powerful and fierce tribe of Zulus.

It was into this depopulated country, that Retief led the Dutch settlers to make friends with Dingan. He went to Dingan's kraal to obtain from him a grant of land, and was received with every appearance of friendliness. He had sixty men with him; the rest were five days' march behind. But there seemed nothing to fear. Dingan made no trouble; the treaty should be signed next day, if they would return to him. The confiding Dutchmen and Retief returned, entered Dingan's kraal, and accepted his hospitality. They were warned to be on their guard; but "We are sure the king's heart is with us," they answered, "and there is no cause for fear."

Fearlessly the white men sat in the kraal, when suddenly Dingan called out: "Seize them; kill the wizards."

A band of Zulu warriors made for the strangers and killed every one of them, including Pieter Retief. The massacre over, the Zulus started off, at the king's orders, to attack the waggons containing the wives and children of the murdered farmers. These were peacefully sleeping, when the Zulus fell upon them. When morning dawned, 41 men, 56 women, 185 children, and as many servants lay dead at the foot of the Drakensberg mountains. And to-day stands a marble obelisk at Weenen— "the place of weeping"—in memory of the tragedy, which ended the first European emigration into Natal. These cruelties roused the rest of the colonists to action. For the last ten years there had been a little British colony at Port Natal. Now, in the face of a common danger, Boer and Briton joined hands. Tremendous fighting took place, but both Boers and Britons perished, overwhelmed by the superior numbers of Zulu warriors.

After these disasters, the emigrants left Natal alone. They crossed the Vaal and founded Potchefstroom, which was for many years the capital of Transvaal territory. Still it was evident to all that unless the cruel Zulu power was crushed in Natal, that fertile land could never be colonised by Europeans.

In 1838, a Dutchman, Pretorius, was chosen to lead an army against Dingan in Natal. With 400 men and 50 waggons, he crossed the Tugela river, and passing Rorke's Drift, reached a nameless stream, known to-day as Blood River. About Christmas time, they came in sight of Dingan's main army. It was so strongly posted, that to attack it would be madness. They could but entrench themselves and await results. The next day was Sunday. The weather was clear and bright. At early dawn, the great Zulu army approached, to the number of 10,000, and the battle began. For two long hours, the Zulu warriors endeavoured to storm the little Dutch camp; but they were armed with spears and assegais, while the Dutch had firearms, and at last the Zulus turned and fled. But over 3000 dead bodies lay on the ground, and the stream that flows through the battlefield, has ever since been called Blood River.

The victory of Blood River, on December 16, 1838, broke Dingan's power, and the Dutch colonists now began to settle on the land. They built the town of Pieter Maritzburg, naming it after their two dead leaders, Pieter Retief and Gerrit Maritz. The day known as "Dingan's Day" has always been kept by the Transvaal Boers as a public holiday, and will continue to be so under British rule. The deeds of the Dutch emigrants were watched with anxious eyes by England and the Governor of Cape Colony, and on the same day that the Battle of Blood River was raging, the British flag was hoisted over Port Natal. The Dutch, under Pretorius, proclaimed themselves a free and independent people in the Republic of Natalia, and set about forming a Government.

Another event now took place, which brought matters to a crisis. Panda, a half-brother of Dingan and son of the famous Chaka, tried to dethrone Dingan. With a large following, he crossed the Tugela into Natal, and sought the protection of the Dutch colonists against their old foe. Pretorius—still the hero of the Dutch settlers—marched with Panda against the king. Dingan was slain, and Panda acknowledged king of the Zulus. The emigrant farmers had now entirely freed Natal from the fierce power of the Zulus, and secured the friendship of their chief.

England now became anxious about their increasing strength and declaration of independence. She looked on them still as her subjects, for the British Government had decided, however far into the "hinterland" colonists might wander, they ever remained British subjects. So in 1842 she sent a small force to Port Natal, to emphasise her claim to the surrounding country. This step was resented by Pretorius, in the name of the Dutch colonists.

"Break up your camp and quit our territory," wrote Pretorius firmly.

Receiving no answer, he marched with 500 men against the English, and soon the little British camp at Durban was in a state of siege. It would have been forced to surrender, had it not been for the daring ride through ten days and ten nights of a young colonist, Dick King. While the English defended themselves as best they might, Dick King was making his way through darkness and danger to Grahamstown, a distance of 600 miles. There were unbridged rivers to be crossed, savage tribes of natives to be avoided; but young King had a stout heart, and on the tenth day of his perilous ride, he arrived exhausted at Grahamstown with his dismal tidings. In consequence of the news he carried, an English ship arrived off Port Natal with soldiers under Colonel Clœte, and the twenty-six days' siege was soon ended.

A year later the territory of Natal was formally declared to be a British colony. It was a turning-point in South African history. A great number of Dutch farmers settled down quietly under British rule, but the fiercer spirits recrossed the Drakensberg and joined their comrades in the Orange River Colony and Transvaal.

Their story will be told later.

CHAPTER 7

THE STORY OF CANADA

"I listen long,
. . . . and think I hear
The sound of that advancing multitude
Which soon shall fill these deserts."
—WILLIAM CULLEN BRYANT.

WHILE England was planting new colonies in South Africa, let us see how her older colonies in Canada were progressing.

In the year 1759, when Wolfe had conquered on the heights of Abraham, and France had reluctantly ceded her North American territories to England, Canada was, after all, a very small possession, populated by some 60,000 French Roman Catholics.

To-day, right across the map of North America, from ocean to ocean, from the boundary of the United States to the silent regions of the icy Arctic Sea, stretches the Dominion of Canada, Kipling's "Lady of the Snows," England's loyal colony, Britain's granary. Let us trace her rapid growth, learn how she attained her present greatness, and successfully realised the ideal of federation.

A feat of arms had captured Canada, but not the French population in the country. Every man had borne arms against the English; every man regarded the invaders as enemies of God and king. Montcalm himself had said, they would be deprived of their laws and customs, their religion and language.

"If you are conquered by Englishmen," he had told them, "you will have to become English yourselves."

But he was mistaken. England at once passed a famous Act, known as the Quebec Act, which allowed the French Canadians to do very much as they had done before, and with this, they were content. So content indeed, that when the thirteen American Colonies, which afterwards became the United States, declared war with the mother country, the Canadians remained loyal to the British flag. The war over, and the Declaration of Independence made known, a long melancholy procession of loyalist refugees, made their way from the United States to Canada. These, having remained faithful to the mother country, were now denounced as traitors. They were known in Canada as the United Empire Loyalists, and were practically the founders of Ontario or Upper Canada. They settled in Nova Scotia, in Newfoundland, in Prince Edward Island, 10,000 toiled up the St Lawrence; they passed Quebec, they passed Montreal, they reached the shores of Lake Ontario. Captivated by the beauty and fertility of the region, they settled in the wilderness, and Kingston sprang up to commemorate their loyalty. To each United Empire Loyalist was given 200 acres, an axe, hoe and spade, a plough and a cow, and rations for three years. By 1784, some 10,000 loyalists had made their homes in Upper Canada. Such a sudden increase of population made it necessary to readjust the Government, in order to prevent difficulties between the English and French settlers. Accordingly the colony was divided into two provinces, Upper Canada or Ontario, consisting, for the most part, of English, Scottish, and Irish colonists, Lower Canada or Quebec, of French.

It was Christmas Day, 1791. Quebec was brilliantly illuminated, for the new Act was to come into force this day. There was much friction between French and English. Feeling ran high, and a riot seemed inevitable. Prince Edward, Duke of Kent, son of George III., father of Queen Victoria, was in the city. Seeing the danger, he made himself known, and standing in a prominent place he called for silence. Then in pure French he shouted—

"Can there be any man among you that does not take the king to be the father of his people?"

"God save the King!" was the enthusiastic cry.

"Is there any man among you that does not look on the new Constitution as the best possible?"

The loyal shouts were repeated.

"Part, then, in peace," cried the king's son, "and let me hear no more of the odious distinction English and French. You are all his Britannic Majesty's Canadian subjects."

His words acted as magic, and happily for Canada his wise advice has always been followed. To-day English, French, and many another nationality live contentedly side by side, sharing all things alike under a free government. Land having been granted to emigrants in Upper Canada on liberal terms, they flocked thither from the United States, until the population had risen to 30,000. This created a movement westward along the shores of the lakes, and a settlement was made at Toronto, on Lake Ontario, which is now the second city in the Dominion. On these northern shores, the settlers lived in rude abundance. The virgin soil brought forth plentifully, deer roamed in the forest, wild-fowl swarmed in the marshes, while rivers and lakes teemed with fish.

So the years passed on, till 1812, when the United States declared war on England and invaded Canada. The Canadians rose as one man to defend their 1500 miles of frontier, and the Americans gained nothing. With the peace of Europe and the exile of Napoleon to St Helena, a great immigration took place from England, Scotland, and Ireland to Canada. Crowded ships brought thousands of peasants, to make fresh homes in the vast wilderness, until Manitoba was ringing with the settler's axe and the air was black with the smoke of many fires.

So matters continued till 1837—the year of Queen Victoria's accession—when the country broke from a state of simmering discontent, into open rebellion. Beginning among the English and Scottish settlers in Upper Canada, it was no small wonder it should spread to the French of Lower Canada—the "Sons of Liberty," as they now called themselves. While the unhappy colonists were shedding their blood in this armed rebellion, a British statesman, representing Queen Victoria, was sailing westward from England, to suggest a remedy for this unfortunate state of affairs.

Lord Durham arrived at Quebec on May 29, 1838, with much splendour and the brightest prospects. The story of his short administration in Canada is one of the most pathetic in history. He saved Canada, but he died in deep disgrace, before his ability had been realised. He at once began his colossal task in the style of a Dictator. "A very Caesar laying down the lines for the future of a province could hardly have been more boldly arbitrary." He had the leaders of the rebellion transported to Bermuda. Having thus cleared the decks for action, he began to remodel the colony. His task was scarcely begun, when his recall was loudly demanded. He had acted with too high a hand, cried men in England. He must come home at once. Then Lord Durham quietly made his great Report on Canada—one of the greatest state documents in existence to-day. It showed a masterly grasp of the situation, and suggested, that the only solution of the problem was the union of Upper and

Lower Canada into one province. He proposed to make the Canadas self-governing, and he prepared the way for that federal union, which took place in 1867. Then he returned to England, to be bitterly attacked by those less far-seeing than himself. His proud and sensitive nature could ill bear the humiliations forced upon it.

The provinces of Upper and Lower Canada were united by law on July 23, 1840. Five days later, Lord Durham, the man who had saved the country's liberties, died, broken-hearted, at the early age of forty-eight.

CHAPTER 8

THE FUR-TRADERS' LAND

"Follow after—follow after. We have watered the root,
And the land has come to blossom that ripens the fruit.
Follow after—we are waiting, by the trails that we lost,
For the sounds of many footsteps, for the tread of a host."
—KIPLING.

FAR away to the north of Canada lay the vast kingdom of the old fur-traders—that "great lone land," which sleeps for more than half the year, under its coat of snow, beneath the dazzling brightness of the northern sky. Only for two or three months in summer the many streams are unbound, vegetation bursts forth, and the summer green is as intense, as was the wintry whiteness. Here the fur-traders were kings.

As long ago as 1670, a great fur company had been started in England under Prince Rupert, to trade with natives on the shores of Hudson's Bay. It was called the Hudson's Bay Company, and had trading rights over enormous tracts of territory. Throughout these vast unexplored treeless regions around the frozen Arctic Sea, wolves and bears, foxes, otters, martens, beavers, and minks roamed unmolested—save for the few Eskimo, who dwelt on the northern shores. "A skin for a skin" was the fierce motto of the Hudson's Bay Company merchants, who pursued their tasks of purchasing skins of fur from the natives.

For a long time they kept to the coast only, but growing more adventurous, they ventured inland, until on the Pacific coast, in the prairies of the Red River, on the desolate shores of Labrador, floated the red-cross flag of England, bearing the magic trading letters H.B.C. Here they built their forts; and here came the natives, dressed in fur, with their bundles of precious skins to barter to the merchant adventurers. Each skin was carefully examined by the white men, and paid for with English articles loved by the Eskimo. Thus a hatchet, a kettle, half pound of beads, or eight knives, would purchase one beaver skin, while a red coat would purchase five.

So far the merchant adventurers from England held undisputed sway over British North America. But the growth of Canada, under the British flag, brought competition. English colonists from the shores of the great lakes, began to penetrate farther and farther westward, until in 1783, the Montreal settlers founded a rival company, called the North-Western Company.

There was a strange fascination about the life of the fur-trader. It was dreary enough in those scattered forts, rising amid the wastes of snow. But each man was his own king, and the wild life of adventure suited many a restless settler from his far-off home.

"Lords of the lakes and forests," the Montreal fur-traders, with dogs and sledges, bounded merrily over the snow, until often enough they developed into exploring parties.

There was an energetic young Highlander, named Alexander Mackenzie, belonging to the North-Western Company. He started one day from Lake Athabasca and discovered the great river that now bears his name—a river second only to the Mississippi in America. He followed it with difficulty to its mouth, and looked out upon the frozen Arctic Sea. The whole country, watered by the Mackenzie river, now bears his name. A few years later, he discovered the country known to-day as British Columbia. This immense tract of territory was an unknown land, hidden behind the Rocky Mountains, when Mackenzie entered it by its natural gateway—the Peace river. Having reached the Pacific coast, he mixed some vermilion with melted grease and inscribed these words large on a face of rock: "Alexander Mackenzie from Canada by land, July 22, 1793." A few years later another pioneer adventurer from Canada, named Simon Fraser, discovered the great river that races through British Columbia, and bears his name to-day.

So the North-Western Company settlers became formidable rivals, to the old established Hudson Bay adventurers. Constant disputes took place: parties of rival traders fought out their differences with gun and hatchet amid the vast solitudes of snow: the "Red River Massacre" was one of the most notorious of these fierce combats. But at last, in 1821, the two companies adopted the wise course of uniting, and peace reigned once more.

Meanwhile the value of this great lone land, was becoming known and realised. The population of Canada was growing, men were pushing northwards and westwards, farmers from Scotland and Ireland were clearing the forests and growing wheat in quantities, until the fur-traders found themselves being pushed farther and farther northwards.

A cry of gold from the Pacific coast in 1858 brought matters to a crisis. Men who, but ten years before, had rushed to California, now made their way north to British territory. Victoria, the little capital of Vancouver's Island, suddenly awoke to find itself a busy commercial city. Across the desolate wastes of country, men struggled from Canada and all parts of the world. Up the golden Fraser river, they floated in home-made rafts and unsafe canoes in search of the precious metal. Then came the old story. Some settled form of government was necessary. The Hudson Bay Company could no longer administer the country, which England now undertook to govern under the name of British Columbia.

This was the beginning of the end. Other vast territories were ceded to England, to be included in the Dominion of Canada, and to-day, the Hudson

Bay Company's trade is restricted to the rocky coast of Labrador and the desolate shores of the Arctic Sea, where colonisation is impossible.

CHAPTER 9

THE WINNING OF THE WEST

"To the West. To the West,
　　To the land of the free!
　Where the mighty Missouri
　　Rolls down to the sea;
Where man is a man, if he's willing to toil,
And the humblest may gather the fruits of the soil."
　　　　　　　　　　　　—MACKAY.

MEANWHILE the United States were also extending their territory to the westward. Like other healthy settlers in a new country, they set to work to enlarge their boundaries, to found new homes amid the pathless forests, to add states to their Union and stars to their national flag. The original thirteen States lay between the Atlantic sea-coast and the tall Alleghany mountains. The vast tract of uncultivated country beyond, watered by the Ohio, was sparely occupied by Indians only. They resented the advance of the white men, who had to fight for their new inheritance.

One day a colonist from North Carolina, more adventurous than the rest, "put a new edge on his hunting-knife, shouldered his rifle, bade his little family good-bye, and with five companions started off to explore the great lone land beyond the mountains." The adventures of Daniel Boone, the pioneer of Kentucky, would fill a chapter. Encouraged by his example, more and more colonists poured over the Alleghanies: they came from Carolina, they also came from Virginia. Among a party of young Virginians, who dared the unknown, was Abraham Lincoln, grandfather of the famous President of that name. One day, he was busy planting his first crops, with his little six-year-old son beside him, when an Indian, darting out of the forest, shot him dead, and seizing his little Tom, ran off. The two elder sons were working close by, and it was but the work of a moment, to seize the ever-ready rifle and shoot the Indian dead, thus rescuing the small brother.

In a rude log-cabin, the fatherless Lincoln boys now lived with their mother. Their days were spent in felling trees, breaking up the virgin soil, and planting crops. Time passed on. Thomas grew up and married. Then one day, he built himself a raft and floated down the river Ohio, to the country known as Indiana, where he made a new home. Here his little son Abraham spent his boyhood. In cowhide shoes, deer-skin breeches, and a home-spun shirt, the future President of the Republic toiled in the deep solitude of boundless forest lands of Indiana. So the vast spaces, between the Alleghany Mountains and the Mississippi, were colonised, and new states were added to the Union. The great river was invaluable, as a highway for trade, and very soon the colonists cast longing eyes to the rich country, that lay beyond its farther banks. This too they wanted to possess. It was known as Louisiana, named after King Louis XIV. of France; but it had been ceded to the United States by Napoleon for a large sum of money. This vast country stretched right away westward to the Rocky Mountains: it was well watered by the Missouri, the great tributary of the Mississippi, and pioneers were soon flocking into its rich and fertile wilderness.

So state after state was added to the Union, star after star to the national flag.

The colonists had now reached the very borders of Mexico. Mexico, that rich country discovered and conquered by the Spanish Cortes, had just thrown off the hated yoke of Spain and declared her independence. A question now arose about the boundary between Texas, one of the United States and the Mexican Republic, and in 1846 war blazed out on the Texan border.

In the great American army, that now crossed over the Gulf of Mexico to Vera Cruz, was a young cadet named Jackson, who was hereafter to play a large part in the history of his country. Born in the backwoods of Virginia, he had grown up, like young Abraham Lincoln, to till the soil and combat the Indians. Now, at the age of twenty-three, he was called to fight for his country, and right well he performed his task. The Mexicans at Vera Cruz soon surrendered to the superior American force, and the army was free to move forwards. Young Jackson had already been promoted for "gallant and meritorious conduct at the siege of Vera Cruz." It was immensely interesting to him, that the army in which he served, should be marching in the steps of Cortes towards the wonderful city of Mexico. A large body of Mexican cavalry stood ready to oppose their advance, but gallantly they scaled the high mountains beyond Puebla, and beheld the beautiful valley of Mexico lying below. There, beneath the mighty shadow of her snow-capped mountains, stood the Imperial city, just as it had burst on the awestruck vision of the Spanish conqueror, three hundred years before. Victory after victory, won by the Americans over the Mexicans, soon placed the city of Mexico within their grasp. Long the Americans lingered in the beautiful city, all living in peace under the shadow of the Stars and Stripes, till, in 1848 peace was signed. The United States gained Texas, as far as the Rio Grande, New Mexico; territory to the north of Mexico was to be theirs, together with the narrow strip of land, between the Pacific and the Sierra Nevada, called California. And so the American troops marched home.

The United States now stretched from coast to coast, from the Atlantic to the Pacific Ocean, a distance of some 3500 miles.

An important event now attracted the eyes of Europe to this land in the Far West. One day a workman, building a saw-mill near the present town of Sacramento, discovered particles of gold in the mud, and a further search revealed the fact that El Dorado was found at last! As the news leaked out, the excitement in the United States rose to a mania. Multitudes of colonists started forth on the great journey across the continent, and forced their way over the Rocky Mountains. Soon 4000 horsemen and 9000 waggons had gone through the high pass. So great were the perils and dangers, that the "track was marked with skeletons."

Some preferred to encounter the dangers of the sea. They sailed by Cape Horn and landed in the Bay of San Francisco. On the barren hills and shifting sands arose a collection of tents and huts, where lived people from every nation. The city of San Francisco sprang up as if by magic, and grew, until it became one of the most famous cities in the world. The entrance to the harbour is known as the Golden Gate, wherein to-day ride the ships of all nations in the world, for San Francisco is the terminus of the Grand Trunk Railway, which runs to New York.

So the Americans won their land, step by step, state by state, star by star, until to-day the national flag numbers forty stars instead of the original thirteen. It was a long and hard struggle between the Indians and the invaders. The winning of the West is a story of progress and bloodshed, of strife between civilisation and barbarism: it is also a story of daring enterprise and astonishing perseverance, of courage and ceaseless toil, worthy the men, whose forefathers had braved the unknown, in the years that were past.

CHAPTER 10

A GREAT ARCTIC EXPEDITION

"Not here. The white North has thy bones;
and thou Heroic sailor-soul,
Art passing on thine happier voyage now
Toward no earthly pole."
—TENNYSON (Franklin).

To the north of the fur-traders' country lay the icy
Arctic regions. Since the days, when Henry Hudson
had perished among the ice and snow of the far
north, Arctic exploration had been at a stand-still; till
early in the nineteenth century, the old fascination
seized upon men once more. The search had been
by no means confined to Englishmen. Men of other
nations had been at work. The Behring Sea was
named by a Russian of that name: one of the most
famous voyages was made by an American.

Parry, the Champion of the North, and Ross
had both made great discoveries in the frozen
regions of the north, but no one had found the
north-west passage. One—Sir John Franklin—who
had already distinguished himself in Arctic
exploration, was now selected to command two
ships, in order to solve the mystery once and for all.

"I might find a good excuse for not letting you go, Sir John, in the rumour that informs me, you are sixty years of age," the First Lord of the Admiralty had said, when discussing the subject with him.

"No, no, my lord," cried the old explorer with enthusiasm; "I am only fifty-nine."

Two stoutly-built ships, the Erebus and Terror, were selected for the service, and with a crew of 129 men and officers, Sir John Franklin left England for the last time on May 19, 1845. They were all in the highest spirits, fully resolved to set at rest for ever the vexed question, of a north-west passage. A last farewell was waved from the shore, and the Erebus and Terror disappeared from view and were never seen again.

Two years passed away, and no tidings reached England from the Franklin expedition. The ships were provisioned for three years. But the year 1847 passed in silence, giving rise to anxiety. Then a large reward was offered by Lady Franklin to any one, who should bring information of the missing ships. In the summer of 1848, an old Arctic explorer started forth to try and discover the fate of Franklin. He was actually within 300 miles of the Erebus and Terror four months after they had been abandoned, but he returned with no tidings.

Other ships followed. Larger rewards were offered. America took up the search, but all was in vain, public anxiety increased, as ship after ship returned without bringing any news.

It was not till 1854, nine years after the expedition had started, that traces were found of the missing men. An Eskimo was found with a gold cap-band round his head. He was asked where it came from.

"From the place where the dead white men were," he answered.

Pressed for further news, the Eskimo said that four years ago, forty white men had been seen, dragging a boat and sledges over the ice, near King William's Land, their ships having been crushed by the ice. They had found the dead bodies of thirty men, they said; evidently the survivors were too exhausted to bury them.

This information was received with the greatest interest in England. Still the fate of the expedition was undecided. At last Lady Franklin herself fitted out a new expedition. She bought a steam yacht, called the Fox, and gave the command of it to Captain M'Clintock, who had already seen service in the Polar seas.

On July 1, 1857, the Fox sailed with a crew of twenty-five. At the end of the month, she arrived off the coast of Greenland, passed through Davis Straits and Baffin Bay to Melville Bay, where, in attempting to cross over to Lancaster Sound, she was stopped by ice. By the middle of August, the little Fox was firmly frozen into the ice. For 242 days, she drifted hopelessly southward, until April came and relieved her from her icy fetters. Through Lancaster Sound she now bravely steamed, to Beechey Island, where stood the lonely graves of three sailors, from the Erebus and Terror. Here Franklin must have spent his first winter, and M'Clintock erected a memorial, sent out by Lady Franklin, bearing the touching words: "And so He bringeth them unto the haven, where they would be."

Then M'Clintock sailed on through the Barrow Straits, steering south; but the summer was all too short, and the winter of 1858, found the Fox ice-bound in Bellot Straits. The long dreary days were spent in making preparations for sledge expeditions in the spring. By the middle of February, there was enough light for M'Clintock to start off in a sledge, drawn by dogs, along the western shores of a peninsula of North America, called Boothia, after its discoverer Sir Felix Booth.

For fourteen days the explorers travelled over the frozen snow, without meeting a living soul. They were growing disheartened, when they discovered four Eskimo following them. Seeing a naval button on one of them, they at once asked where it came from.

"It came," said the Eskimo, "from some white people, who were starved upon an island in a river."

At last they were on the trace of the lost expedition. That night, they slept in a snow-hut built by the Eskimo, and next morning numbers of natives assembled, bearing relics belonging to the dead men. There were silver spoons, buttons, knives, and sundry other things. They also said, that a ship with three masts had been crushed by the ice near King William's Sound. Further discoveries were soon made. In another Eskimo village, they found silver plate bearing the crest and initials of Sir John Franklin. The natives said there was a wreck some five days' journey off.

"Many of the white men," they said, "dropped by the way as they went to the Great Fish river: some were buried and some were not."

One day, the explorers came upon a human skeleton, lying on its face, half buried in the snow, showing that the Eskimos were right. "They fell down and died as they walked along."

And now their reward was at hand. Hidden in a cairn of stones was a blue ship's paper; it was weather-stained and ragged, but it revealed at last the secret of Franklin's expedition,—that secret, for which the whole world had been waiting for ten long years.

The first record was cheery enough. In 1846, all was going well with Sir John Franklin in command. But round the margin of the paper, another story was written in another hand. Two years had passed: Sir John Franklin was dead, the Erebus and Terror, beset with ice for two years, had been abandoned, nine officers and fifteen men had died. The survivors were starting for the Great Fish river. That was all.

Many more relics were collected. There were cooking-stoves, watches, blankets, naval instruments, there was a well-marked Bible and a copy of 'The

Vicar of Wakefield,'—all these were carefully brought back to England.

But, amid all the tragedy and pathos of the lost expedition, stands out the cheering news of success. Franklin had discovered the North-West Passage, though he had not accomplished it in his ships. He had supplied the missing link, and with him lies the glory of the discovery.

M'Clintock now hastened to England with his great news. And England put up a national memorial to the "great navigator and his brave companions, who sacrificed their lives in completing the discovery of the North-West Passage."

CHAPTER 11

DISCOVERIES IN AUSTRALIA

"There dawned at last a day when all was changed.
The restless overflow of Northern lands,
From Old World thoughts and sympathies estranged,
Winged South their way in bold adventurous bands,
Bearing courageous hearts and vigorous hands
To carve their way to wealth with manly toil,
And plant Dominion in productive soil."
—DANIELL (Australian poet).

WHILE the English were opening up hitherto unexplored country in America—away in Australia, Englishmen were also discovering new lands to colonise.

Since the exploits of Flinders and the brave passage over the Blue Mountains, much had been discovered about the interior of the country. But it was Sturt's famous descent of the Murray river, that induced England to take up the matter of Australian colonisation more seriously. In the year 1830, he was exploring the waters of the Murrumbidgee, fearing that his journey might end like others in some dismal swamp, when "On a sudden," he says in his own graphic language, "the river took a general southerly direction. We were carried at a fearful rate down its glowing banks, and in such a moment of excitement had little time to pay attention to the country through which we were passing. At last we found we were approaching a junction, and all of a sudden, we were hurried into a broad and noble river."

He was in reality a thousand miles from the mouth of the Murray river, which to-day forms the boundary between New South Wales and Victoria. Dangers were before him. To the ordinary risk of being wrecked on unknown rocks, was added the danger of encounter with natives. More than one white man had already been a victim to their fierce attacks. Now suddenly some hundreds collected on the banks to oppose Sturt's passage. In a shallow reach of the river, they gathered in force, howling and brandishing their spears. Let Sturt again tell his own story.

"As we neared the sand-bank, I stood up and made signs to the natives to desist, but without success. I took up my gun, and cocking it, had already brought it to the level. A few seconds more would have closed the life of the nearest of the savages. At that moment I observed four men upon the left bank of the river. One of them threw himself into the water, struggled across to the sand-bank, and seizing one of the savages by the throat, pushed him backwards." The chief was evidently very angry, stamping with passion and shaking his clenched fist in the faces of his tribe. So ended a scene, which might well have cut short the wonderful descent of the Murray river by Sturt. Soon the 600 natives were looking peacefully at the little ship, as she glided on her way down the unknown stream. After a sail of thirty-two days, Sturt heard waves breaking on the shore, and knew that the mouth of the newly found river must be near. But bitter was his disappointment to find that shoals and sand-banks blocked the entrance, and it was impossible to sail farther. He must return against stream to his headquarters. The fight with wind and current was tremendous. The exhausted crew fell asleep at their oars from sheer weariness, some grew light-headed, until on the seventy-seventh day of labour, Sturt and his faithful crew reached the end of their journey.

When the news reached England, there was great enthusiasm.

"A spot has been found," wrote Sturt, "to which colonists might venture with every prospect of success, and in whose valleys, the exile might hope to build himself a peaceful and prosperous home."

"Colonisation is an imperative duty on Great Britain," cried the poet Coleridge confidently. "God seems to hold out His fingers to us over the sea. But it must be a colony of hope—and not of despair."

On December 28, 1836, the first emigrant ship reached the shores of South Australia and anchored off Kangaroo Island. It was indeed to be a colony of hope. Here were no more convicts, unwilling to work, but a healthy band of English men and women, ready to bear their share in cultivating the rich valley of the Murray river. Other ships followed, and some 200 colonists gathered under an old gum-tree, unfurled the British flag, and took possession of the new colony. And to-day thousands of colonists go forth every year on December 28, to the old gum-tree, on the plains near Adelaide, to celebrate "Proclamation Day." The site of the new capital was soon chosen, and called Adelaide, after the wife of William IV. of England, at her own special request.

Not only was South Australia now claimed as British territory, but the neighbouring islands of New Zealand were claimed too, and colonised. "Very near to Australia," said an Englishman, speaking on colonisation, "there is a country described as the fittest in the world for emigration— as the most beautiful country with the finest climate and the most productive soil; I mean New Zealand."

Already adventurers from Tasmania and New South Wales had sailed across and made their homes there, despite much opposition from the natives. In vain did the old Duke of Wellington declare, that "England had enough colonies." An expedition started off from the mother country to settle in New Zealand, and they called their capital Wellington, after the hero of Waterloo.

Meanwhile Australian colonisation was growing apace. Already a small colony was growing into existence in Western Australia. Colonists had made a settlement round the Swan river and built the city of Perth on the western coast. But this little settlement was terribly isolated from the other

colonies in Australia, and in the year 1840, one man made his way right across the great continent from east to west, to see if communication could be established by land between the two.

Eyre, the hero of the expedition, had already made many journeys inland,—some successful, some unsuccessful. He had driven a mob of 300 cattle through unknown country from Sydney to Adelaide, a journey which occupied eight months. He did the same journey again, with 600 cattle and 1000 sheep, in three months, and opened up a new trade-route between the two towns. Then he had sailed to King George's Sound, and led a flock of sheep across 300 miles of unknown country to Perth, thus establishing a trade-route between Adelaide and Perth.

Now he formed the daring plan of establishing, if possible, a trade-route by land across the desert, on the shores of the great Australian Bight—of piercing the continent from east to west. In February 1841 a start was made. The party had already been reduced to John Baxter, "a sound solid Englishman," a black man Wylie, and two companions, pack-horses, provisions, and six sheep. And so Eyre turned his back on home and friends to traverse the thousand miles of hideous waterless desert. It was indeed

"A waste land where no one comes
Or hath come since the making of the world."

Often he had to go for five days without a drop of fresh water. He toiled on over the summit of high unbroken cliffs, at the foot of which broke a sailless sea, blown by furious winds rushing up from the antarctic ice. Horse after horse dropped dead in the sand from waterless misery, the black men complained bitterly and deserted more than once; but Eyre's courage kept the party going.

One night a tragedy occurred, which nearly ended the expedition. They were camping for the night, and Eyre had wandered from the camp with the horses. A cold wind was blowing, scuds drove across the moon, the place was solitary: there were no trees, below roared a rough sea. Suddenly the sound of a gun rang out, and Wylie's voice cried, "Come here! come here!" Eyre ran back in terror, to find the camp had been robbed, Baxter slain, and the two black men had disappeared. He was now alone in the very middle of the Great Bight, 500 miles from help. He looked down at the dead body of his friend and away to the desolate sea beyond—and then in the early morning, he started on again, on, with the new horror of murder dogging his steps. He plodded on another hundred miles, which took a month, so weak had he and Wylie grown, when relief appeared. A French ship hove into sight. Eyre lit a fire to attract notice, and soon a boat was making for the shore, and Eyre—wild, hungry, emaciated—was taken on board and nursed back to life by friendly sailors. Then after another month's walk, he staggered into the English settlement of Albany—his great adventure ended. To-day, the electric telegraph connects Adelaide and Perth by the great Australian Bight.

CHAPTER 12

THE LAST KING OF FRANCE

"And empire after empire, at their height
Of sway, ...
Have felt their huge frames not constructed right
And drooped, and slowly died upon their throne."
—MATTHEW ARNOLD.

LET us turn from the stories of colonisation to Europe again.

After Louis XVIII. had re-entered his capital in the summer of 1815, France enjoyed some years of peace. His death, ten years later, left his brother in possession of the throne, but Charles X. was extremely unpopular. He had the old ideas of despotism, that had already proved so fatal to his country, and a general unrest overspread France. Hoping to gain some popularity, the king sent an expedition against Algiers, on the north African coast. After a struggle, famous in history, the citadel was obliged to surrender, and the victorious French Army entered the city in triumph. Algiers is to-day the largest and most flourishing among the possessions of France. But the glory of this, did little to lessen the growing irritation of the people. The crisis soon came. The king stopped the freedom of the press. Shopkeepers and mechanics at once broke into insurrection. They barricaded the streets, dug up the pavements, and overturned the omnibuses. It was July 27, 1830. Next day, Paris was in a state of siege. The old tricolour flag was hoisted by the Revolutionists, but the king would not give way.

"Suppress the rebellion by force of arms," he said firmly.

The royal troops attacked the citizens. Then they too rebelled, and the people, like an overwhelming torrent, burst into the Tuileries. They sacked the palace, broke the magnificent furniture and hurled it into the Seine. At last the king consented to retract his edict.

"It is too late," they told him coldly; "the throne has fallen in blood."

There was nothing left him now but capitulation and exile. He fled to England, where a refuge was offered him by William IV. The "three glorious days of July" were over. France was at liberty to seek a new king. It was not far to seek. Even before the late king had quitted the soil of France, he heard that his own kinsman, Louis Philippe, Duke of Orleans, had been offered the crown.

Louis Philippe was descended from a younger brother of Louis XIV. His father had perished in the Reign of Terror. Exiled from the country and reduced to great poverty, young Louis Philippe had earned his bread by teaching geography and mathematics in Switzerland. He had wandered in the New World, as well as the Old, until the time was safe for him to return to France once more. During the reigns of Louis XVIII. and Charles X., he had lived in Paris, as a citizen moving among citizens. When the three days of Revolution came, he hid in the woods in fear of his life. He was found, brought to Paris, and warmly received by the old revolutionist, Lafayette. They appeared on a balcony together, with the trio-colour flag, and the multitude shouted applause.

A week later, Louis Philippe was made King of the French. The new "Citizen King," as he was called, was popular with his subjects. He dispensed with court etiquette. Anybody and everybody was admitted to his presence, as is the case to-day, with the President of the United States of America. He himself walked about the streets on foot, in "a greatcoat and round hat, with the proverbial umbrella under his arm, and shook hands familiarly with the people."

But Louis Philippe was not the man, to bring peace and prosperity to restless France.

The news of his accession proved the death-blow to one quiet aspirant to the throne, away in Austria. The young son of Napoleon, once King of Rome, was still living. He still remembered his father's great position, as Emperor of the French, and in his sickly body beat a heart as true as steel. A settled melancholy now took hold of him, though he turned with renewed vigour to his military drill and exercises. Therein lay his only hope for the future. He worked from morning to night, he hardly slept, he ate little. He grew thinner and thinner, more and more white. Till at last in 1832 the short tragedy was ended. The son of the great Napoleon lay dead at the age of twenty.

Another man now became the head of the House of Napoleon. This was Prince Louis Napoleon, the son of that Louis Bonaparte who had married Napoleon's step-daughter Hortense and become King of Holland. Prince Louis had been an exile from France for many years, but soon after the death of his young cousin Napoleon, he went to England, where he watched closely the events in France. He watched the growing discontent with Louis Philippe, noted the frequent attacks on his life, his unpopularity with the people.

One summer day, in 1840, he engaged a steamer to take himself and a party of friends from the English coast on a "pleasure trip" to Boulogne. They landed on the coast of France early in the morning, and marched into the town. The Prince, carrying his hat on the point of his sword, shouted "Vive l'Empereur." But the old cry inspired no enthusiasm among the fisher-folk of Boulogne. The only answer was cries of "Long live the King." The soldiers were called out and the Prince had to swim for his life, towards the English ship, for safety. He was caught and brought back, to be imprisoned in the castle. After five years he escaped and returned to England.

Soon after his escape, matters in France reached a crisis. The Citizen-King was a failure. The people cried for reform. They announced that a great Reform banquet should take place in February 1848. Louis Philippe forbade it. The people were exasperated. Tumults ensued. Once more, the streets were barricaded, shops closed, and firing took place in the streets. History repeats itself. The King would not believe the rebellion was serious. He still hoped to restore order. But the insurgents would be satisfied with nothing less, than a complete change of government now. Louis Philippe was seventy-five. It was not likely he would change much.

The Queen, in whose veins flowed the blood of Maria Theresa, faced the situation bravely.

"Go," she said—"Go and show yourself to the troops. I will place myself in the balcony, with my grandchildren and my princess daughters, and I will see you die in a manner worthy of yourself, of your throne and of our common misfortunes."

The king put on his uniform, mounted his horse, and taking his two eldest sons, he rode slowly forth among the sullen crowd. But he was too late. The cry for reform burst forth from every side. He returned in despair. The mob was advancing on the Tuileries. He must abdicate or die.

He seized his pen. "I abdicate in favour of my grandson, and I trust he will be more fortunate than I."

That little grandson was but ten, his father, heir to the throne, having been thrown out of a carriage and killed, but a short time since.

The Act of Abdication was read to the people.

"It is not enough—the whole dynasty must go," they cried.

The work of Louis Philippe was done. He now took off his uniform, laid his sword on the table, put on a plain black coat, and gave his arm to the queen. The sight of the aged couple, with their whitened hair, now going into exile, broke down many a courtier, and, amid stifled sobs, the king and queen made their way from the Tuileries. They crossed the same path, which had been crossed by Louis XVI. and Marie Antoinette fifty-nine years before. Daughters, daughters-in-law, and grandchildren went a different way to avoid detection. Two carriages awaited the royal pair at the gate. But the queen had borne all she could, and, overcome by long agony, she fainted. Tenderly the king raised her and lifted her into the carriage. Disguised, they made their way to the sea-coast, where for some days they lay concealed in painful suspense. Day after day, tempestuous storms made the crossing to England impossible. At last they were able to go, and, under the name of William Smith, Louis Philippe and his queen arrived in England, where, two years later, death ended his tragic career.

France now became a Republic for the second time, and Prince Louis Napoleon became President for a time, after which he was proclaimed Emperor, with the title of Napoleon III.

CHAPTER 13

LOUIS KOSSUTH AND HUNGARY

"I was the chosen trump where through
Our God sent forth awakening breath.
Came chains? Came death? The strain He blew
Sounds on, outliving chains and death."
— LOWELL (Kossuth).

THE flight of Louis Philippe from France, was the "signal for long pent-up fires to break out all over Europe."

Already Belgium had revolted. She had never rested under her union with Holland, as decreed by the Congress of Vienna. William I., King of Holland, had treated Belgium, as a conquered country. And, inspired by the example of France, Belgium rebelled, until her independence was acknowledged by all the powers, and Leopold of Saxe-Coburg was made King of Belgium.

The next to awake was Hungary, the beautiful country between Russia and Italy, of which the great Hungarian poet sings—

"If the earth be God's crown,
Our country is its fairest jewel."

Austria had ruled Hungary for 300 years, not by right of conquest, but by the free choice of the Magyars, as the people called themselves. Emperors of Austria had been crowned kings of Hungary at the capital, Buda-Pesth, on the fast-flowing Danube. But a long line of kings had gradually swept away from the Hungarians, their share in the government: taxation bore heavily on the peasants, and the court of Vienna allowed no freedom to the press.

It was at this moment, that one man arose to be the voice of the people. The career of Louis Kossuth, the Hungarian patriot, is one of the most romantic in history. In the year 1837, when the cry for reform was first making itself heard, he started a little newspaper, which he sent round by special messengers to people in the outlying districts, of his large country. His name was already known to his own people, for the large part he had taken a few years before, when a terrible outburst of cholera spread terror through the land. Wherever the plague was most deadly, young Kossuth had appeared, allaying fear and calming excitement.

His newspaper and ideas of reform did not please the court of Vienna, and one evening, when he was walking alone in the capital, he was seized, blindfolded, and hurried off to the great fortress of Buda-Pesth, where he was thrown into a dungeon.

He spent two years there in total solitude, without books and without friends.

"It was two years of my life lost," he used to say afterwards; "but it was all my life gained."

The popular agitation in Hungary was growing from strength to strength. The release of Kossuth was demanded, and granted by Austria. Pale, worn, and broken, the prisoner came forth to find himself a popular hero, escorted through the streets by a thousand torch-bearers. He now returned with fresh enthusiasm to his newspaper, which was the organ of the new movement. The storm grew. Louis Kossuth became more popular daily. The Hungarian Parliament met in 1847, and Kossuth made his famous speech on the liberties of Hungary. He demanded equal taxation for rich and poor alike, he called for a restoration of ancient rights and liberties.

The report of his speech reached Vienna, the same day with the news of the flight of Louis Philippe from Paris. A storm of excitement swept over Vienna, when Louis Kossuth arrived at the head of a Hungarian deputation to the Emperor. He was hailed with enthusiasm, and lifted high in strong arms above the crowds to the royal palace. At last he stood before his Emperor. At that moment the destiny of Austria was in his hands.

"Be just to my Fatherland, and I will give peace and tranquillity to Vienna," said Kossuth.

The Emperor was terror-stricken. With the news from Paris ringing like a knell in his ears, with the wild shouts of his subjects echoing round the palace, he granted every request, and formed a new ministry for Hungary.

But even while the new Government was planning reform for Hungary, the Emperor was breaking his promises at Vienna and intriguing against his people. In vain Kossuth tried to avert war. In vain deputations went to Vienna to pray the Emperor's mercy. The peril of the moment awoke Kossuth's power and eloquence. With the liberties of Hungary at stake, he assented to the inevitable call to arms. He was no soldier, but his country must be fought for.

"I demand 200,000 soldiers and the necessary money for the war," he cried at last, amid breathless silence, at the end of a long speech in Parliament.

Before these last words had echoed through the hall, four hundred men had risen to their feet, and, raising their right arms to heaven, cried in a voice of thunder—"We grant it—Liberty or Death!"

"You have all risen to a man," answered Kossuth with tears in his eyes. "I bow before the nation's greatness."

The nation was now fully aroused. Volunteers poured into the capital from the hills, valleys, and plains. Old men of sixty, lads of thirteen, flocked to the Hungarian standard. They came with knives, scythes, and hatchets—undrilled, untaught, unofficered. A force so ill-equipped seldom faced an enemy in the field before.

"Hungarians," cried Kossuth, now civil and military governor of Hungary, "there lies the road to your peaceful homes and firesides. Yonder is the path to death, but it is the path to duty. Which will you take? Every man shall choose for himself. We want none but willing soldiers."

As one man, the whole army shouted in answer, "Liberty or Death!"

It is impossible to follow the battles that now took place. Ten times the Hungarians defeated the Austrian army. Then the tide turned. Austria turned to Russia for help, and a great Russian army came slowly marching toward the frontiers of Hungary. Still Louis Kossuth never lost heart. He worked with ever-renewed energy. But it was all in vain. 200,000 Russians and 70,000 Austrians marched into Hungary, and there was nothing left but capitulation.

From this time Hungary is blotted out from the list of nations. Many of her leaders were shot; others, with Louis Kossuth, escaped across the frontier. It is said, before his unwilling departure from the desolate land of his birth, he knelt down and kissed the green grass. Then lifting his voice, he uttered his pathetic farewell to Hungary.

"Pardon me, my Fatherland, me who am condemned to wander about far from thee, because I strove for thy welfare. Oh, poor Fatherland, I see thee bent down with suffering: thy future is nothing but a great grief. Magyars, turn not your looks away from me; for even at this moment my tears flow only for you. Thou art fallen, truest of nations. Thou art no more a nation. Be faithful; pray for thy liberation. God be with thee, my beloved Fatherland. Believe, love, and hope."

Then, toil-worn and broken-hearted, the patriot passed into Turkey. Such was their admiration for his gallant fight for liberty, that the United States sent a steamer to convey him to America. On the way, he visited England, where he was received with great enthusiasm.

"England is great and glorious and free," he used to say.

Louis Kossuth lived on in Italy till 1894. He lived long enough to see Hungary a free country, though not independent of Austria. The Emperor-King, Francis Joseph, who had already ruled Austria for nineteen years, ascended the throne of the newly formed Austria-Hungary dominions in 1867, and from this time peace and prosperity have reigned in the land.

CHAPTER 14

THE CRIMEAN WAR

"All the world wonder'd."
—TENNYSON.

RUSSIA had helped Austria to quiet discontented Hungary. She felt therefore that Austria would stand by her, through any scheme of foreign conquest, she might pursue. Since the days when Peter the Great had made his country famous, every Tsar had cast longing eyes towards Turkey, with its world-famed capital Constantinople. In the beautiful harbour of the Bosphorus, a Russian navy could lie peacefully at anchor, with numerous possibilities before her. Such dreams of greatness, now filled the head of the Tsar Nicholas. Turkey was woefully weak. The Turkish empire was dying, thought the Tsar.

"We have on our hands a sick man—a very sick man," he now told England. "The sick man is dying. We must come to some understanding."

He suggested that England should take Egypt and Crete, while Russia would undertake to protect the Turkish provinces in Europe. England rejected the proposal. A Russian fleet in the Bosphorus would endanger her route to the East.

But matters reached a crisis in 1853. The Turkish fleet was lying at anchor in the Black Sea, when the Russian fleet bore down upon it, destroyed the ships, and killed 4000 Turkish sailors. The news raised a universal outcry in Europe, and within a few months, England and France, on behalf of Turkey, were at war with Russia. They determined to attack Russia in the Crimea. Here at Sebastopol, lay her great naval and military headquarters, here was her key to the Black Sea. But the land, which the allied armies were about to invade, was as unknown to them, as it had been to Jason and the Argonauts when they voyaged thither in search of the Golden Fleece. They landed in September 1854 near a spot, where the river Alma flows into the Black Sea, without opposition from the Russians, who were posted in great strength on the heights across the river.

The English were commanded by Lord Raglan, a man of sixty-six. He had been among the first to mount the breaches at the storming of Badajoz; he had lost his right arm at Waterloo.

The Commander-in-Chief of the French forces was Marshal St Arnauld, able, brilliant, and heroic, but smitten of a mortal disease, of which he soon died.

"With such men as you," he said to his generals, "I have no orders to give. I have but to point to the enemy."

The allies crossed the Alma under deadly Russian fire and scrambled up the heights, amid a searching rain of musketry. Their desperate courage alone won the day. They stormed the Russian position, till the Russians broke and fled. It was the first great European battle since Waterloo. Then English and French stood opposed to one another—now they stood together, and victorious, against the Russians.

They now turned to Sebastopol, hoping to attack it by land and sea at the same time. But a brilliant idea had already occurred to the Russian genius, General Todleben, who was defending Sebastopol. Under the very eyes of the allies, he sank seven Russian war-ships in the entrance of the harbour, till only the tops of their masts were visible. This prevented any attack by sea, and the allies marched on to Balaklava, into whose harbour their ships could sail with safety.

It was yet early on the morning of October 25. Fleecy clouds hung about the low mountain-tops, the blue patch of sea beyond Balaklava, shone in the morning sun, while flashes gleamed from the masses of armed men in the plains. At half-past ten, like a grey cloud, the Russian cavalry galloped to the brow of the hill, that cut the Balaklava plain in two. In all their pride and glory, they swept along the heights, while the British waited breathlessly below. Lord Raglan stood on a hill, overlooking the plain. The battle had already begun, when he sent down a young officer, named Nolan, with a message, that the cavalry must attack at once.

"Attack? Attack what? Where are the guns?" cried the bewildered recipient of this order.

Nolan threw back his head, and pointing to the line of Russians on the heights: "There, my lord, are the Russians; there are your guns."

The order was given to Lord Cardigan, the commander of the Light Brigade. He was startled. Never had such a thing been asked of cavalry before, never had man been told to lead his soldiers to such certain death. He must cross a mile and a half of open plain under deadly fire. He knew there must be a blunder, but discipline forbade him to question.

"The Brigade will advance," he said, casting his eyes over his splendid body of cavalry.

The men too were startled by the order. But it was—

> "Theirs not to make reply,
> Theirs not to reason why,
> Theirs but to do and die:
> Into the valley of Death
> Rode the six hundred."

Suddenly right across the front of the galloping Brigade, rode a horseman, waving his arms madly and crying out words they could not hear. Nolan had discovered the deadly blunder—but it was too late. Another moment, he was shot down, and on

"Into the jaws of Death,
Into the mouth of Hell
Rode the six hundred."

Scourged by a cross fire from the Russians, men and horses fell thick. Still the Brigade never checked speed, never faltered. With steel flashing above their heads, and a British cheer that wrung the hearts of those that watched, they rode to within eighty yards of the great Russian battery. They dashed between the gleaming cannon, and cut down the gunners as they stood. Then through clouds of smoke, the few survivors made their way back—

"All that was left of them,
Left of six hundred."

When the little band of heroes had formed up, Lord Cardigan rode forward: "Men," he cried, "it is a great blunder, but it is no fault of mine."

"Never mind, my lord," was the brave answer; "we are ready to go again."

All Europe, all the world, rang with wonder and admiration at the useless, but splendid charge. Lord Raglan owned with pride, that it was perhaps the finest thing ever attempted. While from the French general were wrung the immortal words, "It is magnificent, but it is not war."

This was but one incident in the battle of Balaklava, in which the Russians were again defeated.

The battle of Inkerman followed a few days later. For nine long hours on a Sunday in November, the battle raged through rain, darkness, and fog, till once again the allies were victorious, the Russians defeated.

Meanwhile the siege of Sebastopol was lingering on. Winter was rapidly approaching. On November 14 a violent storm wrecked twenty-one ships in Balaklava Bay, and the warm clothing and blankets for sick and wounded men, went to the bottom of the sea. Snow followed, and the sufferings of the English and French soldiers were intense. Men were frost-bitten in the trenches outside Sebastopol; they had tents for shelter, rags for clothing, and insufficient food. It was no wonder they died by hundreds and thousands.

Their bitter cry reached England, and she responded readily. Florence Nightingale, with a little band of nurses, made her way to Constantinople and thence to Scutari, where the great Turkish barracks had been turned into a hospital. The story of her wonderful work among the sick and dying soldiers is well known. Hitherto the soldiers had been nursed by orderlies, often ignorant and rough, though well-meaning. Now, for the first time, women undertook the work, which they have managed ever since. Well indeed might the American poet Longfellow exclaim, as he pictured the "dreary hospitals of pain," the "glimmering gloom," and the English woman, with her little lamp softly passing from bed to bed, while the "speechless sufferer" turned to kiss her shadow, as it fell on the darkened walls:—

"A Lady with a Lamp shall stand
In the great history of the land."

Through that long winter, the siege of Sebastopol dragged on, though the trenches were growing nearer and nearer to the doomed city. With the return of summer, fresh efforts were made to take it, and two famous assaults on the Redan and Malakoff forts were repulsed by the Russians. At last, on September 8, the French succeeded in taking the Malakoff fort, and the fate of Sebastopol was sealed. Skilfully and silently, the Russians crept from the town, and retreated by a bridge of boats, blowing up their forts and sinking their boats, leaving the city, they had defended so splendidly for 349 days, like a second Moscow, in flames.

So the Crimean War ended. Russia's dreams of possessing Turkey were ended too for the present, and the Black Sea was declared neutral, its ports being thrown open to every nation.

CHAPTER 15

THE INDIAN MUTINY

"This ballad of the deeds
Of England and her banner in the East."
—TENNYSON.

ENGLAND was resting and recovering from her losses in the Crimea. She was just going to keep her hundredth anniversary of Plassey, when, like a "thundercrash from a cloudless sky," came the news of a mutiny in India, destined to shake British authority in the Far East to its very foundations. When the mutiny broke out—in May 1857—no one in England realised the discontent, that was growing among the dark-skinned natives of distant India. The large kingdom of Oude in the north, had just been brought under British rule to save it from the cruelty and oppression of its native rulers. This was bitterly resented by the natives. They saw the old state of things passing away; they feared for their religion. The English, they said, wanted to make them Christians.

Matters reached a climax at last. Hitherto the native soldiers, known as sepoys, had used a musket popularly called "Brown Bess." In 1857 Enfield rifles were substituted, with greased cartridges. The news spread, that these new cartridges were greased with hog's lard, and it was forbidden for Mohammedans to touch the fat of swine. A panic of religious fear ran from regiment to regiment, from village to village, town to town.

Early in May, a regiment near Delhi refused to bite the new cartridge. The men were tried, and eighty sepoys sentenced to ten years' imprisonment. The following Sunday, when the English were at church, the prison was broken open and the mutinous sepoys were set free by their companions. Then all took up arms, fired on their officers, and marched forth in battle array for Delhi. Here they proclaimed a descendant of the Great Mogul, Emperor of India. Europeans were massacred, and Delhi was in the hands of the mutineers, who held it till the end of September.

Meanwhile mutiny was breaking out in other parts of northern India. At Cawnpore there were some thousand Europeans, of whom more than half were women and children. Under the command of Sir Hugh Wheeler, an old man of seventy, hasty entrenchments were thrown up, and for three weeks, the few defenders held out gallantly against the mutineers, led by the infamous Nana Sahib.

On promise of a safe-conduct across the Ganges, to Allahabad, they at last surrendered, wholly unsuspicious of treachery. Accompanied by sepoys, a long procession of men, women, and children, carrying their sick and wounded comrades, made their way slowly to the boats, prepared for them. Hardly had they embarked, when a murderous fire opened upon them from either bank, from which four men only escaped. For 125 women and children a crueller fate was reserved.

Hearing that General Havelock and an English army were on their way to Cawnpore, Nana Sahib gave orders for an instant massacre of the helpless women and children, who, dead and dying, were cast into a well, the site of which is marked to-day by Marochetti's beautiful white marble angel. Nana Sahib escaped after this and was never heard of again.

Meanwhile at Lucknow, some forty miles distant, a strong man, Sir Henry Lawrence, was coping with the coming rebellion. For the defence of the Europeans, he chose a large building, known as the Residency. With unremitting toil, he laid in stores of grain, powder, and arms, while the defences were strengthened by night and day.

It was sunset time, on the last day of June, when a large body of rebels dashed over the bridge and swarmed into the city of Lucknow. All the Europeans withdrew into the Residency. The blaze of watch-fires and the flash of guns lit up the darkness of the night. It was the first long night of the famous siege of Lucknow. Two days later, Lawrence was in his room at the top of the Residency, when a shell crashed through the wall and burst.

"Sir Henry, are you hurt?" cried a friend, who was with him.

There was silence for a time. Then in a firm voice came the answer—"I am killed."

He was right: the wound was fatal. With his dying breath, he planned for the defence of the Residency, for the safety of his countrymen, now in such peril and distress.

"Never give up, I charge you. Let every man die at his post."

Speaking to himself, rather than to those around him, he murmured: "Here lies Henry Lawrence, who tried to do his duty," words, which may be seen on his tombstone to-day, in Lucknow. They form a simple summary of "the noblest man that has lived and died for India."

Lawrence had calculated, that Havelock and his relieving army, might arrive in another fifteen days. But a fortnight after his death, they had only just reached Cawnpore. No easy task had been allotted to Havelock. Already he had marched 126 miles in nine days, under the burning July sun, fighting four actions with large native bodies in his way. He must have reinforcements before attempting the relief of Lucknow. Pitiful, indeed, grew the messages from the little garrison. If help did not reach them soon, they must fall. They were nearly starving, and the sick were increasing daily. Still Havelock was delayed. Suddenly came the news that another man, Sir James Outram, had been appointed with troops to relieve Lucknow, instead of himself. It was a crushing blow. He had done all that man could do, in the face of obstacles. Now another was to enter Lucknow at the head of fresh troops and win the glory, he had earned. But Outram was too great a man for this.

"I shall join you with reinforcements," he said; "but to you shall be left the glory of relieving Lucknow, for which you have already struggled so hard."

Such an act of self-sacrifice has not been beaten in the noblest days of chivalry. It is one of the bravest acts in history, and won the unbounded admiration of the whole world.

The relieving army now started at once, Havelock at the head, Outram a volunteer in the army. On September 25, they reached Lucknow. It was the eighty-seventh day of the siege. With feelings of joy, they detected the tattered English banner still waving from the roof of the Residency, showing that British hearts still beat within, and they were not too late to save the garrison. Hour after hour they fought the rebel host, till at last they gained the narrow streets leading to the Residency, and in the dusk of that September evening, a deafening shout at last greeted them, as they grasped the hands of their comrades after their brilliant defence.

Lawrence had bade them hold the Residency for fifteen days.

"Hold it for fifteen days? We have held it for eighty-seven!" they might well have cried, in the words of the poet Tennyson.

Meanwhile desperate were the doings at Delhi. The siege, begun on June 4, was not ended till September 20, just five days before the relief of Lucknow.

"If there is a desperate deed to be done in India, John Nicholson is the man to do it." Such was the popular idea among men, who knew the power of this famous brigadier.

The "desperate deed" was truly at hand: Delhi must be stormed. And to John Nicholson was entrusted the post of honour and danger. He—"the Lion of the Punjab"—lead the storming columns, against the defences of the city. Four columns were to assault four of the gates leading into Delhi at the same time, Nicholson himself leading the first column. At first all went well. But after a time, the enemy's fire became so appalling, that the men could not steel their hearts to follow their dauntless leader any further. In vain he strove to nerve them for the last fatal rush onwards; officers and men were falling every moment. At last Nicholson himself strode forward. He turned to his men, and waving his sword above his head, pointed to the foe in front, entreating them to advance. His tall and stately figure, standing alone and unprotected, was an easy mark. In another moment he had fallen, shot through the chest. He was carried from the action, a dying man. He lived just long enough to hear that

Delhi was taken, after five days' heavy fighting—long enough to know, that he had not given his life in vain. He was but one of the many brave men, who helped to restore the authority of England in India; but his name is loved and feared still in the northern provinces of India, where "Nicholson's God" and "Nicholson's Queen" are reverenced to-day. The natives say that the hoofs of his war-horse are to be heard ringing at night, over the Peshawar valley, and until that sound dies away, the Empire of the English will endure.

With the advent of Sir Colin Campbell, as Commander-in-Chief of India, the final capture of Lucknow and Delhi and further fighting, the rebellion ended. England had been taught a lesson. An Act was at once passed for the better government of the mighty Indian empire. The East India Company ceased to exist, and in 1877 Queen Victoria became Empress of India.

CHAPTER 16

THE AWAKENING OF ITALY

"Awake,
Mother of heroes, from thy death-like sleep."
—WORDSWORTH.

ITALY, since the famous days of old, had been wrapt in sleep. The land of Dante was dead, as far as Europe was concerned. She was only a name, only a "geographical expression." The Italians were practically the slaves of Austria. At the famous Congress of Vienna, the land had been parcelled out into dukedoms and provinces, "like so many slices of a ripe Dutch cheese."

Let us tell the wonderful story of her awakening.

When she yet lay in the fetters of Austria, early in the nineteenth century, one man—the pale, fiery-eyed Joseph Mazzini—arose from among the people. And he saw, as no other saw at this time, the vast possibilities that lay before her. As a child, he had wept tears of pity for his fellow-countrymen in poverty or trouble; as a young man, he fancifully dressed in black, mourning for his dead country, whose woes had taken such deep hold of him. The task of Italy was not yet done, he told himself, she must yet arise from her glorious past and speak to nations "the gospel of humanity." A tremendous sacrifice was required. To make a new Italy meant war with Austria; it meant loss of thousands of lives, exile, prison, and misery. Men could only face it at the call of duty. So Mazzini taught his countrymen, and out of his teaching and enthusiasm sprang the society known as "Young Italy."

"Young Italy," he says, "is a brotherhood of Italians, who believe in a law of progress and duty, and are convinced that Italy is destined to become a nation."

As a nation, this mission was given them by God; God's law of progress promised its fulfilment. "God and the People" was the watchword of the new society, which by the summer of 1833, numbered some 60,000 young Italians. Amongst them was Garibaldi, the man who was later to play such a large part, in the liberation of his country.

But the founder of Young Italy was by this time an exile, and taking refuge in England, the land that has never refused shelter to the political outlaws of foreign countries.

"Italy is my country, but England is my home," he used to say in after days.

As the years rolled on, Italy grew more and more determined to throw off the yoke of Austria. In 1848, the second French Revolution broke out. It was followed by the Hungarian rebellion; and the enthusiasm of Italy now burst forth in all its newly-found glory. At Milan, after five days' heroic struggle, the Austrians were driven out and Venice won her liberty. From mountain and valley, town and village, volunteers poured forth to enlist under Garibaldi. Mazzini himself hurried home to enrol as a volunteer, and carry the flag bearing his own watchword—"God and the People."

> " 'Italia Una!' now the war-cry rang
> From Alp to Etna: and her dreams were done,
> And she herself had wakened into life,
> And stood full-armed and free: and all her sons
> Knew they were happy to have looked on her,
> And felt it beautiful to die for her."

Events now moved fast. The northern states threw off the yoke of Austria; the Pope fled from Rome on February 9, 1849; a Republic was proclaimed, directed by Mazzini himself. But Austrian power was yet strong. Neither the enthusiasm of a Garibaldi nor the lofty ideal of a Mazzini, could save Italy at this moment. On March 23 a battle was fought at Novara, in northern Italy, between the Austrians and Italians. With the latter, Charles Albert, King of Sardinia, had thrown in his lot, only to be utterly defeated. When evening fell, he called his generals around him and abdicated his crown.

"This is your king," he said miserably, as he bade farewell for ever to his young son, Victor Emmanuel, who knelt weeping before him. So saying, he passed from his kingdom and journeyed alone to exile and death. He did not live to see that son crowned the first King of United Italy.

Meanwhile Prince Louis Napoleon and most of the French people took up the cause of the Pope, and sent an army to Rome. In the face of danger, Mazzini's little Republic stood firm.

"Rome must do its duty and show a high example to every people," he said.

And heroically Rome prepared to resist overwhelming odds. The "Eternal City" was defended by Garibaldi and his fierce band of volunteers. They were dressed in red woollen shirts and small caps—a strange company, with their long beards and wild black hair. The first shot was fired, and "a thrill of deathless passion ran through Rome." Week after week Garibaldi and his band kept the well-disciplined French army at bay. But the end was certain. At the last, Rome sullenly surrendered, and the French army entered into possession. But not before Garibaldi with his faithful 4000 followers had started off on his famous retreat. It was the last desperate venture of men, who knew not how to yield to the foe. On a warm night in June they left the fallen city.

"Hunger and thirst and vigil I offer you," Garibaldi had told them, "but never terms with the enemy. Whoever loves his country and glory may follow us."

And into the darkness of the summer night rode the red-shirted band with Garibaldi, Anita his wife, and Ugo Bassi, his faithful monk-friend. Foot-sore, hungry, and weary, they made their way amid the Tuscan hills, until they reached the Appenines, into whose depths they plunged. Eagerly they tried to reach Venice, but, driven to the coast and surrounded by the enemy, Garibaldi was obliged to put to sea. He landed again, only to be hunted over mountain and plain. His wife died in his arms. The faithful Ugo Bassi was captured, but Garibaldi escaped from his pursuers at last and retired into silence, till the next crisis of his country's history called forth his most heroic efforts.

CHAPTER 17

KING OF UNITED ITALY

"I write of days that will not come again,—
Not in our time. The dream of Italy
Is now a dream no longer; and the night
Is over."
  —MRS HAMILTON KING (The Disciples).

DARK indeed was the outlook in Italy, when Victor
Emmanuel of Sardinia took up the sceptre, that his
father had flung aside, after the battle of Novara.
The year of revolution had come and gone, leaving
the country more hopeless than ever. But Mazzini
had not lifted his voice in vain, though the prospect
was of the gloomiest, as he sat amid the ruins of
Rome, after the departure of Garibaldi. "He waited
for friends to rally round him, but none dared to
rally; for foes to slay him, but no man dared to slay."
And at last he went his way into exile once more.
His work for Italy was done.

Ten years passed away, and war with Austria
again became inevitable. Instead of the lofty
dreamer, Italy had now a practical man of affairs in
Count Cavour to lead her. His idea was to drive the
Austrians from the country, by force of arms, and

establish a united northern kingdom under his master Victor Emmanuel. But he saw clearly that Italy could not succeed single-handed. So he turned to France, and the Emperor Napoleon agreed to come and help.

War was declared in 1859, and at Genoa, Victor Emmanuel met his new ally Napoleon.

"I have come to liberate Italy from the Alps to the Adriatic," said the Emperor confidently, as together the two monarchs made their way to the front. They carried all before them. The victory of Magenta was followed by that of Solferino, and then, for some unknown reason, Napoleon stayed his hand. He met Francis Joseph, Emperor of Austria, at Villafranca, and made a peace, which filled the Italians with dismay, for it gave the province of Venice to Austria, making union impossible. Cavour was terrible in his anger and grief.

"Before Villafranca," he cried, "the union of Italy was a possibility: since Villafranca, it is a necessity."

The events of 1859 had brought Garibaldi to the fore again. He had been summoned before Cavour. Wearing the historic red shirt, he presented himself at the door and demanded audience of the great Italian minister. He refused his name, and the servant, alarmed by his fierce appearance, refused him admittance. At last, as Garibaldi refused to go away, Cavour was consulted.

"Let him come in," said the minister. "It is probably some poor beggar with a petition."

Such was the first meeting between the great statesman and the no less famous volunteer. Garibaldi now fought against the Austrians, and at the sudden termination of the war, he was hailed as a national deliverer throughout the country. He was now to win yet higher fame.

Sicily and Naples were ruled by one king, and Sicily now raised the standard of revolt, declaring her intention of joining Italy in her struggle for unity. Garibaldi determined to join them with his volunteers.

"Italians," ran his proclamation, "the Sicilians are fighting for Italy. To help them with money, arms, and men is the duty of every Italian. To arms, then! Let us show the world, that this is truly the land once trodden by the great Roman race."

He waited for no orders in this rash undertaking. "I know," he wrote to Victor Emmanuel, "that I embark on a perilous enterprise. If we achieve it, I shall be proud to add to your Majesty's crown a new and glorious jewel."

It was a calm moonlight night in May, when the red-shirted band stole away from the shores of Italy in two steamers, under the command of Garibaldi, bound for Sicily. When fairly out to sea, Garibaldi planned his coming campaign. On May 11, the thousand landed at Marsala.

"Sicilians," cried Garibaldi, "I have brought you a body of brave men. To arms all of you! Sicily shall once again teach the world, how a country can

Garibaldi stood up in his carriage.

be freed from its oppressors by the powerful will of a united people."

The name of Garibaldi acted like magic. Sicilian peasants flocked to his standard, till his numbers were doubled. An army from Naples was now sent to oppose him. The armies met at a little mountain town, called Calatifimi. After a sharp conflict the Neapolitans, in their gaudy uniforms with gold lace and epaulettes, fled before the red-shirted band of half-armed enthusiasts, and Garibaldi entered Calatifimi as a conqueror. Two hundred of his men were wounded, including his son Menotti. Those who knew his utter devotion to the boy, had begged him not to risk so precious a life rashly.

"I only wish I had twenty Menottis, that I might risk them all," was the heroic answer.

On to Palermo marched the liberators. Now they had to creep along goat-tracks on the mountain-side, now they were drenched to the skin by heavy rain, but hungry, shelterless, they trudged on.

"If you join me, you must learn to live without bread and to fight without cartridges," Garibaldi had once told them.

They forced their way into Palermo, and with the capture of Milazzo, they had practically conquered the whole island. It was an achievement, which stands alone in modern history.

Garibaldi now turned his eyes towards Naples. He would yet proclaim Victor Emmanuel king of a united Italy!

As he advanced towards the city, enthusiastic crowds surrounded him. "Viva Garibaldi!" arose from every side, as he made his triumphal entry.

The king of Naples and Sicily had fled, but troops sullenly guarded the royal palace. They waited but one word to fire on Garibaldi. It was an anxious moment. One shot, and the work of the last month was undone. The Liberator stood up in his carriage, and, folding his arms, looked earnestly at the uncertain troops. He was within range of the guns. Amazed and almost terrified, the soldiers suddenly threw aside their matches, and, waving their caps in the air, shouted with the crowd, "Viva Garibaldi!"

Two months later, Victor Emmanuel and Garibaldi entered Naples side by side. Then, having laid this new kingdom of Naples and Sicily at the feet of his king, the simple-hearted chief, refusing all honours and decorations, passed quietly away to his island home at Caprera.

He had fought for Italy and he had conquered. This was reward enough.

Garibaldi outlived Cavour, he outlived Mazzini. All three men had played their part in the union of Italy. For the first time since the downfall of the great Roman empire, one king ruled over Italy, though ten years more passed, before the kingdom was complete and the Italian flag floated over Rome.

It is not the banner of Mazzini's ideal Republic. The attainment of unity fell far short of the high purpose, which inspired Young Italy. But that unity, which once seemed an impossible dream, is to-day an accomplished fact; and it may be, that as her national life develops, Italy will yet prove worthy of her great past and of a yet greater future.

CHAPTER 18

CIVIL WAR IN AMERICA

"Thou too sail on! O Ship of State!
Sail on, O Union strong and great!
Humanity, with all its fears,
With all the hopes of future years,
Is hanging breathless on thy fate!"
—LONGFELLOW.

WHILE Italy was claiming her right to become a European nation, America was fighting to preserve her hardly won nationality. The Union flag, with its stars and stripes, now waved in the breeze from coast to coast. America was one free and independent nation. But storm-clouds were rising dark and terrible over the fair skies of the prosperous Republic.

The Southern States, known as the Cotton Garden of the World, employed a large number of slaves, without which, it was impossible to produce the cotton demanded of them by foreign countries. The Northern States had long since abolished slavery, which was unnecessary to them, and they now urged the Southerners to do the same. Such a measure meant ruin to the South, and it was stoutly opposed. In 1852, a story-book called 'Uncle Tom's Cabin' came out: it painted a dark picture of the cruelties of the slave-holders and the misery of the slaves, and created a profound impression throughout the reading world. Feeling ran high as men spoke of the burning question: Should the slaves be freed in the Southern States?

In 1859 one old man took matters into his own hands. John Brown hated slavery, and one dark night, he entered Virginia with a small body of men, seized Harper's Ferry, and called on the slaves to rally round him and fight for their freedom. But John Brown was captured, tried, and hung, for his raid was illegal, if well-intentioned.

"This is sowing the wind to reap the whirlwind, which shall soon come," said the poet Longfellow, with prophetic vision. He was right. John Brown's death raised excitement over the slave-trade to fever heat, and three years later, the men of the North were marching to battle, to the solemn chant—

"John Brown's body lies a-mouldering in the grave,
But his soul goes marching on."

The following year, Abraham Lincoln, our little colonist friend of Indiana, had been elected President of the United States. How step by step he had risen from log-cabin to the White House at Washington, is a well-known story. Tall and thin, with sad dreamy eyes, as sorrowing for his country's troubles, "slow to smite and swift to spare," he now stood to address the vast crowds, eagerly awaiting his inaugural address.

"We must preserve the Union at all costs," he cried emphatically. "The question of slavery must remained unsolved for a time."

But it was already too late. The Southern States had taken the law into their own hands. They had declared themselves independent of the Union, and elected a President of their own. The deed was done. War was inevitable now. If the Union was to be upheld by Lincoln, it must be by force of arms. He appealed to the country for men and money. The response was enthusiastic.

> "We're coming, Father Abraham,
>   six hundred thousand strong,"

sang the men of the North as they marched under the Union flag. Boys of fifteen sat down and cried, if they were refused to serve with the colours.

Fifteen southern states, including Virginia, now took up arms against the whole North. The end was certain. But the opening battle, fought near the high-banked stream of Bull's Run, near Washington, ended in a victory for the South. It was early on the morning of July 21, 1861, that the first shots of the Civil War were fired. Before evening, the undisciplined army of the North had melted away.

One name was made famous on this day. Through the heat of that cloudless summer day,

Jackson had fought with the bravest—cool, fearless, determined. At one moment, when men were wavering and hearts beginning to fail, there was a cry: "There's Jackson standing like a stone wall."

"Stonewall Jackson!" shouted the soldiers; and Stonewall Jackson was the idol of the Southern army, till the day he fell, accidentally shot by his own men.

The North now rose in its full strength. General Grant took command of the Northern army and gained a great victory at Shiloh, Tennessee, though the loss in men was terrible, exceeding 22,000.

Then the Southerners turned their eyes to the sea. They constructed a ship, that was to open a new era in naval warfare. For the Merrimac was the first iron-clad vessel in the world, that ever steamed to battle. The Southerners sent her forth to destroy the wooden navy of the North in Chesapeake Bay. She had already begun her work of destruction, when a yet stranger sea-monster was seen, ploughing its way through the stormy waves, from New York, to try its strength against the Merrimac. The Monitor, too, was an iron-clad. She had been built in hot haste, by the men of the North; but so grotesque did she appear, that she looked just like a "cheese-box on a raft." She steamed alongside the giant Merrimac, and the first battle between iron-clad ships, in the history of the world, ended in the destruction of both. From this time the old wooden three-decker was doomed.

Meanwhile Lincoln, suffering deeply at the White House, Washington, took one of the most memorable steps in American history. He declared that all slaves were free from January 1, 1863, in those States still rebelling against the Union. "The sun shall shine, the rain shall fall, and the wind shall blow upon no man, who goes forth to unrequited toil," he said, as he took his final stand against Southern slavery.

The South fought with renewed strength. Now that slavery was abolished, their struggle became desperate. Under such leaders as General Lee and Stonewall Jackson,—the "soldier-saints" of the South,—they fought hard and long.

But a heavy blow now befell the South in the death of Stonewall Jackson, who fell mortally wounded at Chancellorsville. Amid darkness and confusion he was shot by his own men by mistake at the moment of victory. For days he lay dying in the Southern camp, and men almost grudged the victory that was costing them so dear, though 18,000 Northerners lay dead and wounded on the field of Chancellorsville.

As the "soul of the great captain passed into the peace of God," an outburst of grief rose from the stricken people.

"It were better for the South had I fallen," said Lee pathetically, as he realised his loss.

Meanwhile, at the White House, Lincoln was in despair at the news of the losses at Chancellorsville.

"My God! my God! what will the country say?" he cried, with tears streaming down his cheeks.

From this time onwards the cause of the North prospered. Jackson was dead and he could not be replaced, while overwhelming numbers from the North swept through the Southern States. The city of Atlanta in Georgia had been seized, and now Sherman—one of the heroes of the North—proposed his famous march to the sea. He would take 60,000 men through the very heart of the enemy's country and seize their sea-coast towns. The risk was tremendous, and many were the voices to shout that "Sherman's dashing Yankee boys would never reach the coast." But off they started in high spirits, like schoolboys on a holiday, cutting a swathe sixty miles broad as they went. They destroyed the railways through Georgia, and finally reached the coast, capturing the important strongholds of Savannah and Charleston. This was followed by the capture of Richmond, the Southern capital, and the great surrender of General Lee and the army of the South.

The great Civil War was at an end. It had carried mourning into almost every family in the United States, it had cost 600,000 lives, but it had decided once and for all that the United States of America was one nation, without slavery in its midst.

For four years, Abraham Lincoln had guided the Ship of State, through stormy seas, and he had steered her into calm waters at last. Peace was declared early in April 1865. A few days later, the

President paid for it with his life. It was a tragic end to the great war.

Lincoln was in the theatre at Washington, when he was shot through the head by a man from the South. Striding on to the stage, the murderer brandished his knife, and with one loud cry, "The South is avenged!" he vanished from sight.

A mighty wave of grief burst over the Republic. The man who had freed four millions of slaves, preserved the Union, and given peace to his country, could ill be spared at such a moment.

Sorrowfully they bore him back to his old home 2000 miles westward.

"Thy task is done: the bond are free:
We bear thee to an honoured grave,
Whose proudest monument shall be
The broken fetters of the slave."

CHAPTER 19

THE MEXICAN REVOLUTION

"New occasions teach new duties;
        Time makes ancient good uncouth.
They must upward still and onward,
        who would keep abreast of Truth.
Lo, before us gleam her camp-fires,
        we ourselves must Pilgrims be,
Launch our Mayflower and steer boldly
        through the desperate winter sea,
Nor attempt the Future's portal
        with the Past's blood-rusted key."
                        —LOWELL.

THE American war had spent its passionate fever, and the title of United States was no longer a mockery, when Napoleon III. set out on his crazy expedition to conquer Mexico. Heedless of the Monroe doctrine, which decreed "America for the Americans," he landed a French army on the shores of Mexico, and declared the country to be an empire. He persuaded the Archduke Maximilian of Austria and his wife Charlotte, daughter of the King of Belgium, to become emperor and empress of his new empire.

There is nothing more pathetic in history, than the tragedy of these two young lives. The young couple started forth on their ill-fated journey in the highest spirits, and were crowned Emperor and Empress of Mexico in 1865, amid some semblance of enthusiasm. A French army protected them, and Napoleon himself found money to build a gorgeous palace at Chapultepec, where they kept open court for a time. But when the Civil War was ended in America, the United States refused to recognise the new Mexican empire, and Napoleon was obliged to withdraw his troops. Thus deserted, there seemed nothing left the young Emperor Maximilian, but abdication. He took up his pen to sign away his empire, but his wife seized his hand.

"I will go to Europe," she cried, "and make a personal appeal to Napoleon."

The interview with Napoleon in Paris was long and heated. In vain the young empress wept, in vain she pleaded for the empire. Napoleon refused to help. The strain proved too much for the heartbroken empress—she lost her reason, and, though yet alive, has never realised her husband's fate. Finding that his wife's efforts were in vain, Maximilian lost heart, and realising the hopelessness of his position, surrendered to the Mexican authorities.

"I am Maximilian, Emperor of Mexico," he said proudly, as he gave up his sword.

"You are a Mexican citizen and a prisoner," was the rough answer.

He was tried and shot. The Mexican tragedy was ended.

A new Mexico has now arisen on the ruins of the past. In 1876, Porfirio Diaz was elected President of the Mexican Republic, and under his wise and capable rule, Mexico has awakened and strengthened herself to take her place among the nations of the world. Six times has Diaz been elected to the Presidency, and to-day he lives in the palace, which the unfortunate Empress Charlotte had loved, and which Maximilian had adorned for her enjoyment at the expense of France. Civilisation has advanced with rapid strides, and two great railway lines already connect her with the United States, which country had stood by her through her darkest days.

The year 1881 was an eventful one in the history of the United States, for in it, President Garfield began and ended his short term of well-won office. Like Abraham Lincoln, James Garfield rose from a log-cabin to the White House at Washington, occupied by the President of the United States of America. He was born in the Ohio wilderness, where his parents had cleared a tract of land and built a log-hut. One summer day, the dry leaves and branches in the adjacent woods caught fire, and fearing for his crops of ripening corn, James Garfield's father, by tremendous exertions, stayed the fire and saved his little homestead. But, weary and overheated, he took a chill and died in the prime of manhood, leaving his widow and four small children to struggle on, as best they might.

The future President was a year and a half old at this time. At three he was sent to a little school in the district; at four, he had received a prize for being the best reader in his class. At eight, he had read every book within his reach. His outdoor life made him a very giant of strength, and it was soon recognised that young James Garfield stood mentally and physically above his fellows. He earned money as a carpenter, as a labourer, as a canal-hand, so that he might educate himself. Few men ever worked harder than the future President of the United States. With cheerful perseverance, he taught himself Latin, Greek, and mathematics. At last he had earned enough to go through college. He took the highest possible honours, and was made President of the Hiram College in Ohio. An enthusiastic teacher, it has been said of him that "he revealed the world to the student and the student to himself."

Wider fields of activity soon claimed him. In 1860, he was elected a member of the Ohio Senate, where, though by far the youngest member, he soon distinguished himself. The great conflict against slavery was raging in the Northern States. Lincoln was President, and the South had risen to arms. On the declaration of war, Garfield sprang to his feet in the Senate and moved enthusiastically, "That Ohio contribute 20,000 men and 3,000,000 dollars" to the State. Taking command of a regiment himself, he soon proved as victorious in war as he had been successful in times of peace. After faithful service in the Civil War for over two years, he entered Congress, and soon became a prominent member.

The crowning honour of his life came in 1881, when he was elected President of the United States of America. For four short months, he showed himself worthy of his high post; then he was shot by a disappointed office-seeker, and the whole nation broke into mourning.

James Garfield was a man of whom America might well be proud. Upright, steadfast, hard-working, true as steel, he grew from boyhood to manhood, until he became an example to all peoples and all nations. The words he used of others are true of himself: "The victory was won, when death stamped on them the great seal of heroic character, and closed a record which years can never blot."

CHAPTER 20

FOUNDING THE GERMAN EMPIRE

"What is the German Fatherland?—
Is it Prussia? Is it Swabia?
Is it the grape-hung Rhine?
Is it the Baltic gull-sought strand?
Greater, O greater—the German Fatherland."
—ARNDT.

THE rise of the German Empire is one of the most striking events of the nineteenth century; and its founder, William VII. of Prussia, stands forth strong, simple, capable, "a man among men, a king among kings, and a true father to his people," the first emperor of a united Germany.

Born at Berlin in 1797, twenty-fourth in direct descent from that young Conrad von Hohenzollern, whom Barbarossa, 600 years before, had singled out for a position of trust,—young Prince William and his elder brother grew up amid the gloom of the overshadowing power of Napoleon. At the ages of eleven and nine, already dressed in Prussian uniforms, the little princes watched the Prussian army marching to do battle with Napoleon. The news of their disastrous defeat at Jena, must have been for ever impressed on their childish minds.

"Ah, my children," their mother the queen had cried amid her tears, "you cannot understand the great calamity that has befallen us. Do not content yourselves with shedding tears, but some day strive to be great generals. Conquer France and retrieve the glory of your ancestors. Prove worthy descendants of Frederick the Great."

Napoleon entered Berlin, and the king, Frederick William III. of Prussia, fled with his queen and the young princes.

"We have lived too long under the laurels of Frederick the Great," the queen cried in despair, as she lay dying soon after, broken-hearted at her country's troubles. She did not live to see that famous day, when her two sons fought their first battle against Napoleon on French territory, and entered Paris in triumph with the Tsar Alexander of Russia and the Emperor of Austria. While Napoleon was escorted to his exile at Elba, and the Austrian Emperor took his daughter and the little King of Rome to Vienna, the young princes were shown Paris by Baron Humboldt, after which they visited England.

Events followed quickly. The Congress of Vienna reinstated the German princes in their little independent states. The battle of Waterloo followed. Then came the marriage of Charlotte of Prussia to Nicholas, afterwards Tsar of Russia, when Prince

William had to hold the diadem over his sister's head, for three whole hours during the marriage ceremony. His own marriage followed, then the death of his father and accession of his brother, as King Frederick William IV. of Prussia.

It was not till the year 1861, that William became King of Prussia on the death of his brother without heirs. He was now sixty-four. He had been in the Prussian army over fifty years. His eldest son, the Crown Prince, had married the Princess Royal, daughter of Victoria Queen of England; and their son, the present Emperor of Germany, lay in his cradle.

The new king set to work at once on schemes of reform. Prussia had lost her place among the nations of Europe; she had been humiliated because her sword was rusty in its scabbard, she had been slighted because her army had degenerated. The strength of the army must be increased. In future the Prussian army must be the Prussian nation in arms.

"If you wish for peace, be ready for war," was the motto of the great soldier Moltke, who was William's right hand.

At the head of the ministry, he placed Otto von Bismarck, destined to become one of the greatest statesmen of modern times—the man, who did more for Prussia and the union of Germany, than the king himself.

"The German problem," he asserted in a famous speech, "cannot be solved by parliamentary decrees, but by blood and iron."

"Blood and iron" were soon to play their part in the coming struggle for unity. In 1863, the crown of Denmark passed to Christian IX., father of Queen Alexandra of England. For numbers of years the neighbouring states of Schleswig and Holstein had been subject to Denmark. They were mostly peopled by Germans, and William of Prussia now declared they should be independent. Denmark refused, and war broke out. Austria joined Prussia, and together the two giant nations attacked poor little Denmark. The Danes fought like heroes, but they were crushed by overwhelming numbers.

The war over, Austria and Prussia quarrelled over their prey. The King of Prussia and Bismarck coveted Holstein: they pictured their great war-ships riding at anchor in the splendid harbour of Kiel. The quarrel grew. William was personally attached to the Emperor of Austria, and greatly disliked the idea of war. But the iron will of his minister Bismarck overcame all scruples, and the "two giant brothers, Austria and Prussia, began to feel for their swords and shake their gauntleted fists at each other."

The German states took different sides. Saxony, Bavaria, Wurtemburg, Baden, Hesse, and Hanover fought for Austria. The northern states fought for Prussia. The armies met in Bohemia, on Austrian territory. The king, Moltke, and Bismarck were all there when the great battle of Sadowa or Königgrätz was fought.

"It was one of the saddest moments of my life, when I crossed the boundary of your country as an enemy," said William afterwards to the Austrians. "I have not come to make war upon peaceable citizens, but to defend the honour of Prussia."

The campaign of 1866 has special interest, as being the first war carried on under modern conditions. The organisation of the Prussian army, and their use of the needle-gun as opposed to the old muzzle-loader, awoke the world to a revolution in military science.

Sadowa was fought and won by the Prussians on July 3, 1866.

"Your Majesty has not only won the battle, but the campaign," said Moltke truly.

But the old warrior-king was searching the battlefield for his son, the Crown Prince, whose final charge with the Prussian Guards had driven the Austrians from the field. Father and son met at last, and with the tears running down his furrowed cheeks, the king took from his breast his own Order of Merit, and gave it to the Crown Prince.

The Seven Weeks' War was over. The results were momentous. Peace was made, by which Austria accepted her utter exile from Germany, and Prussia annexed Hanover, part of Bavaria, Schleswig, and Holstein.

And to-day, right across the Prussian province of Schleswig-Holstein, runs the famous deep-cut canal, sixty-one miles long, connecting the mouth of the Elbe with the bay of Kiel. It was opened by the present German Emperor in 1895. It saves 600 dangerous miles of sailing round the stormy north of Denmark's coast, and to-day in the famous harbour of Kiel, is building Germany's navy.

CHAPTER 21

THE FRANCO-GERMAN WAR

"Heirs no more of others' glory,
But the makers of their own."
—TRENCH.

THE victory of the Prussians at Sadowa, startled the French Emperor Napoleon III., and set all France in a ferment. This growing power of Prussia, this union of the northern German states, must be stopped— the unity of Germany prevented at all costs.

For the next few years the storm-cloud hung over France and Prussia, only to burst in 1870, when war was declared by France. Never did a nation rush so headlong upon its fate, than did France in that fateful July. She had yet to discover that the Grand Army of Napoleon I. existed no longer.

Within a fortnight of the ultimatum, the wonderful machinery of the Prussian army was in perfect order, and half a million men stood at the frontier fully equipped for the coming war. In the face of a common danger, many of the southern German states had thrown in their lot with Prussia. The last days of July found William, the old warrior-king, now seventy-three, bidding good-bye to his white-haired Queen, as he left her for his last campaign, while Napoleon was leaving the Empress Eugenie in Paris and hastening with his only son, the young Prince Imperial, to the Franco-German frontier.

While William King of Prussia was taking over the command of the splendid army, created by himself, Napoleon was experiencing bitter disappointment, as he too placed himself at the head of the French troops. For the truth was dawning upon him, that the French army had degenerated, and that it was totally unprepared to carry on a great war.

In the first battle, fought at Saarbrücken, a small Prussian town just across the frontier, the young Prince Imperial received his "baptism of fire," displaying a coolness and presence of mind worthy the name he bore. The victory was with the French. It was their first and almost their only success in their unfortunate contest. A few days later, a victory was won by the Prussian Crown Prince on the heights of Wörth, and on the same day the Germans defeated another French army at Spicheren. Within a week, the French armies were in full retreat towards Metz, whither they were being forced by the Prussians.

Napoleon, now ill, disappointed, broken, resigned his command to Marshal Bazaine. Matters fared no better. By the middle of August, after severe fighting, Bazaine, with 70,000 French soldiers, was shut up into Metz and communication was cut off.

Meanwhile Paris was in a state of wild consternation. Marshal Macmahon, sent with a large force to the relief of Bazaine at Metz, was forced by the enemy towards Sedan, into the beautiful valley of the Meuse. Napoleon and the Prince Imperial, after driving hither and thither, had reached Sedan at midnight on August 30. Their outlook was hopeless enough. By masterly strategy, the Germans had surrounded Sedan by an iron circle.

"Soldiers," pleaded Napoleon in broken tones,—"Soldiers, prove yourselves worthy of your ancient renown. God will not desert France if each of us does his duty."

The morning of September 1 broke through dense mist. The battle began early.

While William, King of Prussia, with Moltke and Bismarck, watched the fight from the top of a neighbouring hill, the Emperor Napoleon was exposing himself recklessly, hopelessly, wherever the fight was hottest. As the day wore on, the struggle continued, and the Prussian ring of fire closed in more and more hotly round the gallant Frenchmen. It is impossible to describe that fateful day of Sedan. Macmahon was wounded early in the morning, and disorder prevailed among the French troops. In a confused and hopeless mass, the French fought heroically: they were almost sublime in their despair. At last all was over. At five o'clock, a white flag of truce was borne to the King of Prussia from

A Meeting took place between William of Prussia and Napoleon III.

Napoleon, shouts of "Victory, Victory," rent the air; but it was in a broken voice that the old king read aloud the few heart-broken words, addressed to him, by his fallen foe: "Not having been able to die in the midst of my troops, there is nothing left me, but to render my sword into the hands of your Majesty."

The capitulation of Sedan was complete. An unconditional surrender was demanded by Prussia. A meeting took place between William of Prussia and Napoleon. The contrast between the two men was very great. William, notwithstanding his burden of seventy-three years, was tall and upright; his keen blue eyes were flashing; there was the glow of triumph on his fresh cheeks. Napoleon was suffering deeply: his eyes drooped, his lips quivered, as he stood bareheaded and weary before his German conqueror. His sun had set for ever. His career was ended. After some detention in Germany, he went to England, where, with the Empress Eugenie and Prince Imperial, he made a home at Chislehurst till 1873, when, broken-hearted, he died.

Meanwhile Paris was in a state of revolution. When Bismarck demanded the provinces of Alsace and Lorraine, with the fortresses of Strasburg and Metz, France stoutly refused.

"Not one inch of our territories, not one stone of our fortresses will we surrender," cried the French people.

In less than a week after Sedan, two German armies began rolling their "waves of men" towards Paris, and the city prepared for a siege. "Like some gigantic clock whose works have broken, social life, industry, trade, business, had suddenly come to a stand-still, and there remained but one passion—the resolution to conquer." Everywhere men were in uniform, being equipped and drilled; Paris had become an immense intrenched camp.

On September 19, 1870, the siege of Paris began. Three weeks later the King of Prussia entered Versailles, and the palace of Louis XIV. became his home for the next five months. Paris had now no means of communication with the outer world, save by balloons. One day, Gambetta—now Dictator of the French Republic—escaped from the besieged city in a balloon. There is a story, that, as the balloon passed over the Prussian and German armies, amid the clouds and the birds of the sky, William turned to Bismarck.

"What is that black speck in the sky?" he asked.

"It is a minister," replied Bismarck. "It is the heroic Gambetta on his way to Tours, where he will assemble battalions."

He was right. Gambetta collected an army and marched against the enemy, only to be defeated near Orleans. A greater disaster yet, was in store for the unfortunate French people. On October 27, Marshal Bazaine surrendered at Metz, and his 70,000 men and vast stores of war-material fell into the hands of the Germans. It was a cowardly act, for which he was afterwards tried and sentenced to death.

Meanwhile, inside Paris, famine was threatening. Since the middle of October, meat had been rationed. In December, not a beast remained of the great droves of oxen and flocks of sheep, which had been turned into Paris in September. Horses were being slaughtered. Winter came on, with unusual severity. Balloons ascended into the cheerless wintry sky with their freight of carrier-pigeons, despatches, and letters, bearing news of suffering and misery to the outer world. December came and went. The New Year of 1871 dawned drearily. The sorties of the besieged were unsuccessful. At last 40,000 horses had been eaten. Dogs, cats, and rats fetched high prices. The death rate increased rapidly. With the advent of January, all shops shut and the streets grew deserted. Yet in all their misery, the Parisians would not tolerate the idea of surrender.

Meanwhile, under the influence of German triumphs on the battlefield, an idea of German unity had seized the minds of the German people. State after state had joined the union, and now the moment had come, to declare the old King of Prussia, Emperor of United Germany, of which Prussia would be the head.

He was at Versailles, when this supreme honour was offered him. As the deputation from the German states entered, the King stood in front of the great fireplace in full uniform, wearing all his well-won decorations.

On his right stood the Crown Prince, on his left, the princes of the new empire. The voice of the old white-haired monarch trembled with emotion, as he accepted the great position. On January 18, he was proclaimed Emperor of Germany at Versailles.

The following day, the men of Paris made their last desperate sortie on a large scale, but thousands were killed and the rest driven back to the now starving city. It was the beginning of the end. "Capitulation had become a brutal necessity." Pitifully, hopelessly, Paris awoke to the bitter truth. In January the last shot was fired. Paris had surrendered. By the treaty of peace Alsace and Lorraine, with Strasburg and Metz, were to be ceded to Germany. France recovered quickly, and has lived in peace under her Republic ever since.

And the old King of Prussia made his triumphant entry into Berlin, as Emperor of Germany, amid cheers that rent the air. Bismarck and Moltke, and his beloved son, the Crown Prince, were with him, to share in his enthusiastic reception.

"Hail, Emperor William! Hail to thee and to the brave German host thou leadest back from victory!" ran the words on the banner, that floated from the statue of Frederick the Great.

So united Germany hailed its conquerors, and to-day the grandson of William reigns over a German Empire, which has grown yet stronger since the eventful days of Sedan, Metz, and the siege of Paris.

CHAPTER 22

THE DREAM OF CECIL RHODES

"I dream my dream, by rock and heath and pine,
Of Empire to the northward. Ay, one land
From Lion's Head to Line."

—KIPLING.

WHILE France and Germany were fighting out their quarrels in Europe, England was playing a vacillating part in South Africa.

The country occupied by the Boers, between the Orange river and the Vaal, was without adequate central government: the emigrant farmers had a very primitive way of managing their own affairs, and they were continually at strife with the natives.

For this reason, Sir Harry Smith, Governor at the Cape, formally annexed this region, under the name of the Orange River Sovereignty, established an administration under an English resident at Bloemfontein, and withdrew to Cape Town. This was in 1848. But peace was short-lived. The Boer farmers rebelled against British authority, and called on Pretorius to lead them to battle.

There is a story told of the Boer leader, which rivals the heroism of the old Romans. When the messenger arrived to summon him to command the Boers, the wife to whom he was utterly devoted lay dying, and Pretorius refused to leave her. But her courage was equal to her patriotism: "By staying here," she urged, "you cannot save my life. Your countrymen need your services: go and help them."

Pretorius went, and never saw his wife again. He led the Boer army to Bloemfontein; the English resident and his small force surrendered, and the conquering army marched southwards. At Boomplaats, between the Orange river and Bloemfontein, they were met and utterly defeated by Sir Harry Smith himself. The Boers fled hastily across the Vaal river, and the Orange River Sovereignty was re-established.

But further trouble was in store. The powerful tribe of Basutos, under their king Mosesh, made a disturbance on the frontier, which the English resident tried in vain to quell. Pretorius alarmed the English by suggesting the possibility of his joining the Basutos with a Boer army. In these circumstances, and not wishing for further fighting, the English decided to grant independence to Pretorius and his Transvaal emigrants.

On January 17, 1852, in a farm on the Sand river, a document, known to history as the Sand River Convention, was signed, granting to the Transvaal Boers, the right to manage their own affairs apart from England.

Soon after this, Sir Harry Smith sailed away from South Africa. The two towns of Harrismith and Ladysmith keep alive the memory of his energetic work. No sooner had he gone, than the Basutos began to plunder the Orange River Sovereignty. The new governor at once marched an army into Basutoland, but he greatly underrated the strength of the Basutos and the difficulty of transport over the high mountain passes. After some skirmishing the English were defeated, but they had fought so well that Mosesh made peace, and it was decided that the Orange River Sovereignty too must be relinquished.

Another convention was signed at Bloemfontein February 23, 1854, by which the inhabitants of that colony were declared to be a free and independent people. They at once took the name of the Orange Free State.

In this way the two Dutch republics—the Transvaal and the Orange Free State—sprang into existence.

The infant republics at once set to work to form their governments, which consisted of a President and an assembly known as the Volksraad. Under its clever Dutch President, the Orange Free State was peacefully governed. "All shall come right," was the motto of President Brand, words now engraved on his monument at Bloemfontein.

War and peace alternated between Boers and Basutos, till at last Mosesh turned in despair to the English.

"Let me and my people rest and live under the large folds of the flag of England," he prayed.

England listened, and in 1869, she took Basuto-land under her protection, thus establishing her authority from Natal to Cape Colony.

Such was the state of affairs when an event took place, which changed the whole course of South African history.

One day, a trading hunter, saw a child in the house of a Dutch farmer, playing with some pebbles from the Orange river, which had been given him by a native boy. Struck by the brilliance of one of them, the trader examined it carefully, and convinced that it was no ordinary stone, he took it away. It was discovered to be a diamond worth £500. Not long after this, a Hottentot produced a magnificent diamond, which was sold as the "Star of South Africa," for an enormous sum of money. In a surprisingly short time, no less than 10,000 diggers had made their way to the Orange river, and thence up the Vaal, in their search for diamonds. Hundreds of adventurers made their way from Europe and America, turning the quiet life of the colonists into a restless, fevered search for riches. A dispute arose as to the ownership of this rich country. It was necessary for some strong hand to keep order there; so England bought the claims of the Orange Free State, and raised the British flag over the new territory called Griqualand West.

Among the early arrivals at the diamond-fields was a young Englishman, named Cecil Rhodes. He had left the university of Oxford, with signs of advanced consumption, and the doctors had given him just one year more to live. But the dry, clear, rainless air of the veld soon established his health, and he worked hard as a diamond-digger at the mines near the new settlement in Kimberley. Men who knew him in these early days of rough camp-life noted his industry, his ability, and his perseverance. They noted his eagerness, as the Kaffirs hauled up in buckets the diamond-bearing blue ground, beat it into gravel, and handed it to young Rhodes to pick out the diamonds. A few years later, a young Scottish doctor arrived at Kimberley. Dr Jameson and Cecil Rhodes soon became great friends. They lived together, and in long rides over the measureless veld, Rhodes began to unfold his plans to the sympathetic ears of his friend. He had already framed the purpose of his life. The wealth he was acquiring, was but a means to an end, and that end was a vast imperial federation for South Africa. The great Dark Continent, with its almost unknown interior, had already fascinated the delicate dreamy Englishman, who was thus to become the founder of the British Empire in South Africa.

CHAPTER 23

THE DUTCH REPUBLICS IN SOUTH AFRICA

"Later shall rise a people, sane and great,
  Forged in strong fires, by equal war made one,
  Telling old battles over without hate."
                                   —KIPLING.

THE diamond-fields had been ceded to England for a large sum of money, but this had not been done, without public protest on the part of many influential burghers of the Orange Free State. In the Transvaal, the financial embarrassments were greater, and the Zulus under Cetewayo, the successor of Dingan, threatened the frontiers of the state. An English commissioner, Sir Theophilus Shepstone, was sent to Pretoria to arrange matters, and on his recommendation, the Transvaal was once again placed under British rule. There can be no doubt that, however strong his conviction of the necessity of this action, it was opposed to the wishes of the great majority of the burghers, and that no sufficient opportunity was given to them of expressing their views.

On April 11, 1877, in the market-place of Pretoria, he read the proclamation declaring that the Transvaal had passed into the hands of the Queen of England.

For a time after this, all went well: Cetewayo promised peace, the country's debts were paid, trade revived, and pressing needs were relieved. Then came a boundary dispute with the Zulu king, and neither Natal nor the Transvaal was safe.

"Why do the white people start at nothing? I have not yet begun to kill. It is the custom of our nation, and I shall not depart from it."

This was the answer of Cetewayo, when remonstrated with by the English.

Peace was no longer possible, and in January 1879 an English army, under Lord Chelmsford, crossed the Tugela and entered Zululand. Although he had heard of the brave and reckless daring of the Zulus, Lord Chelmsford underrated their strength. On the morning of January 22, he moved out of his camp at Isandhlwana—the "little hand"—leaving it open and unprotected, with 700 Englishmen and some native soldiers. Towards mid-day, the British soldiers saw to their dismay 20,000 Zulus advancing towards the camp in full battle array. There was no thought of surrender. Back to back stood the British soldiers and fired coolly on the Zulu warriors. As long as they had ammunition, they kept the foe at bay. The Zulus fell by hundreds; they "dashed against the few white troops, as the breaking of the sea against a rock." But at last the Zulus overmastered them. "Fix bayonets, men, and die like British soldiers!" It was the last order. One more desperate struggle, and all was over. When Lord Chelmsford returned towards evening, his brave soldiers lay dead on the field of Isandhlwana.

The victorious Zulu army was now free to sweep into Natal. But the Tugela rolled between the black men's country and the white, and at the ford— Rorke's Drift—stood 130 Englishmen under two young officers. On the afternoon of this fatal 22nd, two men came furiously riding from Isandhlwana to Rorke's Drift, with the news of the sudden disaster, which meant that a huge Zulu army was advancing rapidly toward the ford.

In a moment, the young officers had decided to hold the drift at all costs. With biscuit-boxes and sacks of maize, they made their defences as best they could. Two hours later, swarms of Zulu warriors were upon them. All through the evening, the gallant little band kept some 3000 Zulus at bay. Night fell, and still they fought on—fought till four o'clock in the morning, when the Zulus gave up the contest, and the little band of heroic Englishmen stood victorious at Rorke's Drift. They had saved Natal from invasion, they had redeemed the defeat at Isandhlwana.

Strong reinforcements were now sent out from England to break the Zulu power. With a desire to fight under the British flag, and to gain experience in warfare, the young Prince Imperial of France, Louis Napoleon, sailed with the forces.

How the heir of the Napoleons was, one day, overtaken by a band of Zulus, and killed before he could escape, is a tragic story in the annals of the war.

Lord Chelmsford now advanced into Zululand with a large army. The battle of Ulundi was fought, Cetewayo was utterly defeated, and fled from his capital. The power of the Zulus was now broken for ever, the king was taken prisoner, and to-day, Zululand, a small territory on the coast, forms part of the Colony of Natal.

Delivered from the Zulus, the Boers were even more anxious than before to secure their independence. England's uncertainty in the past, led them to hope that she might once more be induced to change her mind; but she refused to withdraw her influence.

A powerful champion now arose to lead the Transvaal Boers. Paul Kruger had driven his father's sheep northwards in the Great Trek of 1836. He had grown up fearless and free, with other farmers' sons; he had hunted and fought with the rest of them, until his courage marked him above his fellows. A field-cornet at the age of twenty, he soon rose to be commandant. He had been chosen one of the three messengers to go to England with the new demand for independence, and he now took a leading part in securing that independence.

On December 16 (Dingan's Day), 1880, together with Pretorius and Joubert, he hoisted the national flag at Pretoria, and proclaimed the independence of the Transvaal. Then the whole mass of Boers rose and attacked the small bodies of English troops scattered through the country. The long-threatened storm had burst. The Governor of Natal, Sir George Colley, raised hurriedly what troops he could and marched northward to relieve the English garrisons in the Transvaal. But his way was barred by a strong force of Boers, under Joubert, at Laing's Nek, the entrance of the pass over the Drakensberg leading from Natal to the Transvaal.

On January 28, 1881, the British troops tried to storm the pass, only to be repulsed with heavy loss. A few days later, on the Ingogo heights, above Laing's Nek, they were again defeated. Sir George Colley, smarting under disaster and failure, and eager to retrieve his losses, now made a plan, which ended in his defeat and death on Majuba Hill.

At dead of night, with some 400 men, he left the British camp and began the long laborious climb up the mountain-side. Dawn was breaking, when they reached the top. Rising high above the ridges of Laing's Nek, Majuba Hill commanded the surrounding country. Below them lay the Boer camp. It was Sunday morning. Suddenly the Boers discovered the British soldiers in their red coats standing against the sky-line on the summit of Majuba. At first it seemed as if the Boer position was hopeless; then some of the bravest among them offered to climb the hill and dislodge the English. Undaunted and unopposed, they climbed upwards, taking cover as they went. It was one of the finest things ever attempted; and the personal bravery of the Boers was beyond all praise. So secure did they feel on the summit of Majuba Hill, that the English had prepared no defences. Suddenly the small Boer detachment stood at the top, pouring a deadly fire upon the English, who were utterly surprised. Entirely demoralised, the British forces broke and fled down the steep sides of the mountain. Sir George Colley was shot at once, and the tragedy was complete.

"The troops fought like heroes," said Joubert simply; "but God gave us the victory."

Then, once more, England changed her mind. Mr. Gladstone was Prime Minister, when it was determined to give back the Transvaal to the Boers, subject to the suzerainty of the Queen. This was in 1881, and from this time, under the Presidency of Mr. Paul Kruger, the Transvaal State pursued its uncertain course till war again broke out in 1899.

CHAPTER 24

LIVINGSTONE'S DISCOVERIES IN CENTRAL AFRICA

"Away—away in the wilderness vast,
Where the white man's foot hath never passed."
—PRINGLE.

THE settlements of the Dutch beyond the Orange river and beyond the Vaal had added considerably to the area of exploration in South Africa. Still little enough was known of the interior. Bruce had explored the sources of the Nile, Mungo Park had found the Niger, a young Englishman had revealed Lake Chad, and a famous Frenchman had explored Timbuctoo; otherwise, little had been done in this direction. Central Africa was a blank, or a "maze of nonsensical geography," until Livingstone, a young Scottish doctor and missionary, opened up a pathway through the mysterious country.

A small mission-station stood at Kuruman, in the heart of Bechuanaland, under the direction of a Scotsman, Dr Moffat. To join him, young Livingstone landed at Algoa Bay in the year 1841, and after a slow ox-waggon journey of 700 miles, he

141

joined his friends. Not long after, he was sent to form a new mission-station at Mabotsa, now included in the Transvaal territory.

Now Bechuanaland, like the rest of South Africa at this time, was infested with lions. One day a troop of lions suddenly appeared, and the young missionary joined the natives in a lion-hunt. Seeing one of the largest sitting on a piece of rock, some thirty yards off, Livingstone fired.

"He is shot! he is shot!" cried the natives; but Livingstone turned round to see the lion in the act of springing on him. It caught him by the shoulder, dragged him to the ground, and crunched his arm into splinters.

The mission-station thrived for a time under Livingstone and his wife, Moffat's daughter, until constant Boer raids made it no longer possible. Fleeing from British rule in Natal, the Boers now looked towards Bechuanaland for the extension of their boundaries. In one raid, they plundered Livingstone's settlement, carried the little black children off as slaves, and the young missionary determined to move farther inland, where white men had never yet been. In June 1849, with his wife, three children, and some natives, he started with oxen and waggons to trek northwards. Journeying through the desert,—a hopeless wilderness of rocks and sand and grey lifeless scrub,—he reached the river Zambesi. But finding no healthy spot for a settlement, he determined to send his wife and children to England and continue his explorations alone.

It was the summer of 1853, before he reached the Zambesi river once more. The journey, even without a wife and family, was tedious and slow; but he was more determined than ever to open up a path to the interior.

"Cannot the love of Christ carry the missionary where the slave trade carries the trader?" he would say. "I shall open up a path to the interior, or perish."

He made friends with the Makololos, who lived about the shores of the Zambesi; and with their help he slowly made his way up the river in a canoe, on and on into the unknown country. Leaving the Zambesi, the little party struck across vast flooded plains, on their way westward to the coast. Food grew scarce, until they were glad enough to eat moles and mice; they had to swim deep rivers and fight their way through dense forests: but Livingstone's resolution never failed. At last, fever-stricken and utterly worn out, he staggered into Loanda, the Portuguese settlement near the mouth of the Congo, to find an Englishman, and once more to lie upon an English bed.

The temptation to sail to England was great, but he felt his work unaccomplished; and after four months' rest, he plunged back once more into the heart of Africa, intending to reach the eastern coast by the Zambesi river. It took nearly a year to reach the Makololos, at Linyanti, once again, and another rest was sorely needed by the exhausted explorer.

His discovery of the Victoria Falls is interesting. The natives had talked to him of some wonderful waterfalls on the Zambesi, near which they had never ventured, on account of "smoke that sounds." Livingstone approached them awestruck, for truly this huge river, nearly half a mile broad, rushed through a narrow crack, and the angry waters foamed and roared a hundred feet below, throwing masses of white spray high up into the sunlit air.

"Being persuaded that we were the very first Europeans who ever saw the Zambesi in the heart of Africa, I decided to name them the Falls of Victoria," says Livingstone in his wonderful journals, which may be read to-day.

With a party of Makololos, Livingstone now started for the last thousand miles to the eastern coast, to the mouth of the Zambesi, Vasco da Gama's River of Mercy. Through rich country and beautiful scenery they passed, as they wended their way through the land since claimed by the English as Rhodesia, till they reached Portuguese territory, and reached the Portuguese settlement of Quilimane by the sea. Here, after four years' wandering, he took ship for England.

The grief of his black attendants at his departure was pitiful. "Take us," they cried; "we will die at your feet."

He agreed to take the chief; but the sea was wild and stormy, huge waves broke over the ship, and the terrified native threw himself overboard and was drowned.

Livingstone landed in England after an absence of sixteen years. He had opened a path right across Africa from coast to coast, and gratefully his country acknowledged his services. He had done much, but much remained yet to be done; and the summer of 1858 found him in the Dark Continent, ready for further exploration.

His faithful Makololos rushed to the water's edge to meet him.

"They told us you would never come back," they cried; "but we trusted you."

Hearing of large lakes to the north, he made his way up the river Shire in a steam-launch, which he had brought from England. Such a snorting and groaning she made, ascending the river, that Livingstone christened her the Asthmatic; but she bore them safely at last to the beautiful mountain-lake, Shirwa, and a few months later to the larger lake, Nyassa, which now forms the boundary between Rhodesia and Portuguese Africa.

"How far is it to the end of the lake," Livingstone asked one day.

"Why, if one started, a mere boy, to walk to the other end, one would be a grey-haired man before one got there," was the native answer.

Time passed on, and Livingstone discovered Lake Bangweolo, to the west of Nyassa, now included in the territory of Rhodesia. Still, though beset with many hardships, weak from fever, faint for want of food, the undaunted explorer pushed onwards to find the lake Tanganyika, already discovered by Englishmen, while searching for the source of the Nile. Onward he struggled, attended by two faithful black men, Chuma and Susi, like the travellers of old, determined to accomplish or die. Sometimes, too weak to walk another step, he was carried on Chuma's back. News reached the coast that he was dead. It was years since he had been heard of alive.

One day, he was sitting in his hut on the shores of Lake Tanganyika, when Susi came running to him crying: "An Englishman! I see him!" Incredible as it seemed, it was indeed true. America had sent out Henry Stanley, afterwards a distinguished explorer himself, to search for Livingstone, and the two men had met in the very heart of Africa.

"You have brought me new life—new life!" murmured the tired old explorer, as Stanley told him all that had happened, during his long absence from news of home and country.

He grew rapidly stronger, and after a time the two explorers started forth together, and completely surveyed the north of Lake Tanganyika.

On Stanley's return to America, Livingstone, turning his back once more on comfort and luxury, set out on his last heroic journey, never to return. He grew weaker and weaker; the crossing of streams chilled him to the bone; tropical rains turned the country into a vast swamp; and, despite the attentions of Chuma and Susi, it was evident the old explorer was dying. One night they went into his hut, and by the light of a dim candle they found Livingstone kneeling by his bedside, his head buried in his hands—dead. Then the faithful negroes buried his heart on the spot where he died—Ilala, on the lake Bangweolo—under the shadow of a great tree in the still forest, after which Chuma and Susi carried the body of their beloved master over hundreds of miles to the coast, braving hardships, hunger, and thirst for his sake, until they could give it into the hands of the English settlers at Zanzibar.

So died one of the greatest modern explorers of Central Africa. The whole Lake region, which he discovered, is now under British protectorate, and civilisation is rapidly being carried forward, for the good of mankind.

CHAPTER 25

CHINA'S LONG SLEEP

"Thro' the shadow of the globe we sweep into the younger day:
Better fifty years of Europe than a cycle of Cathay."
—TENNYSON.

WHILE the great continent of Africa was slowly accepting European civilisation, let us see how the continent of Asia was awakening. China—the "Celestial Empire"—the Cathay of the poets and Marco Polo—a country larger than the whole of Europe, and inhabited by no less than four hundred million human beings,—is one of the oldest nations on the earth. Before Abraham had made his journey from Chaldea to Egypt, this "black-haired" race of Chinese had their Emperor; while Greece was rising on the shores of the Great Sea, Confucius, the Chinese sage and teacher, was writing the history of his country.

"Behold," said the prophet Isaiah, speaking about seven hundred years before the birth of Christ, "these shall come from afar . . . from the land of Sinim," which is China.

Even in these old days of long ago, as to-day, the government of China was very oppressive. Here is a story of Confucius. Seeing a woman crying by a tomb, as if she had suffered from "sorrow upon sorrow," Confucius spoke with her, and found that her father-in-law, her husband, and her son had all been killed on that spot by a tiger.

"Why, then, do you not move from this place?" asked the great teacher.

"Because," she replied, "here there is no oppressive government."

"My children," said Confucius, calling his disciples together, "remember this: oppressive government is fiercer than a tiger."

Such is the reverence to-day for Confucius, that the little Chinese boys with their shaved heads and black tufts of hair, have to bow to the tablet of the ancient sage, as they enter their school of a morning.

Great and clever were the Chinese in the days of old. Before the birth of Christ, they had built the first suspension-bridge in the world, and engineered their famous "Great Wall" of China, sections of which may be seen to-day. This colossal wall stretched in an unbroken line over mountain and plain, it was carried across rivers and over the tops of hills, till its battlements and towers seemed lost in space. 1500 miles long, its paved top formed a roadway, which for long centuries had been daily traversed by long caravans of camels, engaged in traffic between Mongolia, Siberia, and China.

They invented the mariner's compass; they discovered how to make silk; they manufactured the famous porcelain known by their name to-day; their literature was celebrated and printed five centuries before Europe discovered the art of printing; they invented copper coinage, and first used carrier-pigeons to bring home news from their ships.

But, as the centuries rolled on, and other nations absorbed new ideas, the Chinese remained stationary. Emperor succeeded emperor, and dynasty followed dynasty. Then came a day, when the first European penetrated into China, and Marco Polo brought back accounts of the Great Khan or Emperor, who ruled the vast Empire.

In the sixteenth century, Portuguese traders arrived on the coast. One of them made his way to the sacred capital of Peking, where he was instantly beheaded by the Emperor's orders. The Dutch followed, and were more successful, as they obtained leave to come "once every eight years" for purposes of trade. They were followed by English traders. Tea was now introduced into Europe, for the first time.

"I did send for a cup of tee (a China drink), of which I had never drunk before," says an Englishman in 1660.

With English supremacy in India, the British traders brought opium, from the poppy-fields of the Ganges into China, where it soon became very popular. More and more eagerly the natives of China thronged to meet the British opium-ships, till the

Chinese Government forbade them to smoke it in any quantities.

War broke out between the British and Chinese in 1840, and the first Opium War ended in a treaty, which ceded the rocky island of Hong-Kong to England.

But the opium trade continued, and Chinese feeling grew bitter against the "foreign devils," as the Europeans were called. Wars and treaties followed. The English and French together took the Taku forts, at the mouth of the Peiho, which flows through Tientsin, and marched to the sacred capital. Here at Peking, within the walls of the Forbidden City, dwelt the Emperor—the Son of Heaven, as he was called, the ruler of the Celestial Empire. By his orders several Europeans had been imprisoned, and the allies now sought their release. This they obtained, and to impress the Chinese, the troops destroyed the wonderful Summer Palace at Peking.

Meanwhile the Chinese were torn by an internal rebellion, which now assumed very threatening proportions. A village schoolmaster, who thought himself inspired, announced that he was the Heavenly King, and rightful heir to the throne. He collected a band of followers, known as the Taipings; and ever-gathering hosts marched through China, plundering and seizing town after town. The Chinese were terror-struck at the sight of this fierce barbaric band with their tawdry dresses and long, lank, black hair. But there was no regular Chinese army to send against them. So Li Hung

Chang, the most famous soldier and statesman of modern times, turned in his distress to an English officer at Shanghai. And in 1863 Major Gordon came to the rescue. With a quaintly-mixed army of Chinese and Europeans, in green turbans, of some 3000 men, he succeeded in quelling the Tai-ping rebellion. He captured city after city, until gradually the rebels—though three times the number of the "ever-victorious army"—melted away before his brilliant achievements.

It would take too long to tell how this Gordon went into the thickest battle, armed only with a small cane, called by the Chinese his "magic wand of victory"; how the oriental treachery of Li Hung Chang caused him to resign his command; and how he flogged from the room, with his magic wand, the treasure-bearers, who entered his presence with bowls of wealth from the Imperial treasury.

"Chinese Gordon" returned home from this rich country with a yellow jacket, a peacock's feather to be worn in his cap, and four suits of uniform proper to his rank of Ti-Tu, the highest in the Chinese army. It is reward enough for some men to have done their duty.

The years passed on, and China slowly opened door after door to European traders, though still little enough was known of the interior. When the idea of a railway was put before one of the Chinese princes, he answered: "I quite understand that in Europe you should employ iron rails to transport you from one end of your country to another. Here we use waggons. We may not travel so fast, but then we are never in a hurry."

Perhaps it was somewhat natural that China should be behind other countries to adopt railways. She possessed one of the largest rivers in the whole world—the Yangtze or Great River, which was navigable for 1000 miles inland. Hence it was not till 1894 that the first railway was opened from Tientsin to Peking, and this was due to European enterprise.

Gradually, however, Great Britain, the United States, Russia, Germany, and France, obtained rights and concessions, and each country sent a representative to live at Peking. Contact with the West seemed to be working for good, when suddenly in 1900 news flashed over the civilised world that riots had taken place at Peking; that bands of rebels, known as Boxers, who hated foreigners, had laid siege to the Legations; that the German ambassador had been murdered in the street, while numbers of missionaries with their wives and children had been massacred or burnt. Those who knew China well, felt there was little hope for the Europeans shut up in Peking. But after a gallant defence, they were relieved at last from their desperate position. It was all a bitter disappointment to those who had watched with satisfaction the awakening of China.

With her magnificent opportunities, her sea-coast, her excellent harbours, her forests of timber and rich mineral resources, with her thick population of energetic, industrious, and resourceful people,

China may yet rise in the strength of a splendid past, to take her part in the history of the modern world.

CHAPTER 26

THE LAND OF THE RISING SUN

"Step by step we gained a freedom,—
Known to Europe, known to all;
Step by step we rose to greatness."
—TENNYSON.

VERY different to China and her long sleep, is the story of wakeful Japan, that "child of the world's old age."

"The two most wonderful men in the world," said Louis Kossuth, "are Prince Bismarck and the Emperor of Japan."

Let us see how this Emperor or Mikado earned his well-won praise, and how in the short space of thirty years he and his Prime Minister, Count Ito, raised Japan from a state of oriental despotism to a first-class European power,—for it is a feat without parallel in the world's history.

The first knowledge of the Japanese Empire was brought to Europe by Marco Polo in 1295. He had heard of "Chipango," an island in the high seas, 1500 miles from the coast of China—the land of the Great Khan. This was the land of the Rising Sun, whose origin, though shrouded in mystery and legend, dates from the sixth century B.C.

With China, she had resented the interference of foreign traders, and rejected all attempts to introduce Western civilisation. She was as carefully sealed to the outer world, as the enchanter's famous casket. In the midst of the pearly waters of the northern Pacific Ocean, she lay in her self-imposed isolation, while the great world moved onward and upward; while eastward, some 5000 miles across the sea, the United States of America were rapidly becoming one of the first commercial nations in the world.

And so it happened one day in the year 1853, when the Japanese were living "like frogs in a well," they were rudely awakened from their dream of peace and security by the sight of some American war-ships advancing boldly to their coasts.

Commodore Perry had been sent by the United States, with a friendly letter from the President to the Emperor of Japan, his "great and good friend." The letter pointed out how near the two countries were to one another, and how important it was they should be friends and live peaceably together. As the great war-ships ploughed through the peaceful waters, towards the Land of the Rising Sun, the shore seemed alive with startled and wondering inhabitants. The arrival of Commodore Perry, with the President's letter, caused the greatest consternation. Notwithstanding his declaration of friendliness, they trembled before his battle-ships and powerful armaments. At first they indignantly refused to negotiate.

"Never has the clash of foreign arms been heard within the precincts of our holy ground," they cried as with one voice. "Let not our generation be the first to see the disgrace of a barbarian army treading on the land where our fathers rest. Peace and prosperity of long duration have enervated our spirit, rusted our armour, and blunted the swords of our men," they added, with heavy hearts.

The great ships sailed away, and eight months later returned for the answer. Meanwhile war in the Crimea had broken out, British war-ships were in Chinese waters, and the Japanese made up their minds, that they must sign the treaty demanded by the President of the United States. What chance had they against British and American war-ships, with their little fleet, which consisted of one little paddle-wheel steamer, two sailing vessels, and a three-masted schooner?

So the treaty was signed. Japan's beautiful ports were opened to foreign trade; the enchanter's casket was unwillingly unsealed at last. Other nations soon followed the example of the United States, and obtained treaties allowing them to trade. And to their great surprise, instead of barbarians, the Japanese found these foreigners kind and just. Soon after the entrance of the foreigners, a party of Japanese went to Europe; they travelled about from city to city, and returned in two years, astonished with all they had seen and heard.

"It is not the people of the West, who are the barbarians," they exclaimed on landing. "We ourselves are the barbarous people."

And what did the foreigners find in this mysterious country of the Japanese? They found an empire about the size of the British Isles, a group of islands "set in a silver sea," and thickly populated with quaint and fascinating little people. They found a mountainous district, with one volcano—Fujiyama, the peerless mountain—towering above the rest, short rivers and streams racing to the sea, and good harbours. Japan was a land of flowers. Gardening there had been brought to a fine art. From the humblest cottage to the Emperor's palace grounds, grew a profusion of wild roses, camellias, orchids, violets, and lilies, while much skill was lavished on the celebrated chrysanthemum of world-wide fame, as seen to-day in the official crest of Japan. The people themselves were short and very pleasing: they were dressed in long gowns of flowered cotton or silk with broad waist-bands. They wore no hats, but shielded off the fierce sun with fans and parasols. They were much taken up with art, and had brought drawing and painting to wonderful perfection. They were a people of the strictest and loftiest code of honour, light-hearted and happy. Such, briefly, was the Mikado's empire—the land of flowers and sunshine, in the middle of the nineteenth century, when she was forced to open her doors to the outer world.

The country was ruled by the Emperor in name, by the Shogun in deed. This dual control

brought endless confusion, to the newly awakened empire; but it was not easy to abolish, in a moment, the manners and customs of hundreds of years. But the state of things grew unbearable, and at last the Shogun was forced to resign. Somewhat pathetic are his last words.

"I surrender the whole governing power into the hands of the Imperial Court. This is the best I can do for the interests of the Empire."

The resignation of the Shogun was followed by one of the most remarkable events in modern history. The chief land-owners, or feudal lords, who, for generations, had held their lands from father to son, now offered the Emperor all their possessions and all their men. With lofty eloquence, they acknowledged: "The place where we live is the Emperor's land. How can we call it our own?"

Thus at one stroke the lands of Japan passed to the State, and the feudalism of long years was no more.

Japan had awakened. The period of "enlightened peace" had begun.

And to-day, fully aware that their awakening is due to the visit of Commodore Perry in 1853, the Japanese have erected a monument to his memory on the spot, where he first landed in their midst, on that eventful day in July.

CHAPTER 27

JAPAN—BRITAIN'S ALLY

"From East to West the circling word has passed,
Till West is East beside our land-locked blue;
From East to West the tested chain holds fast,
The well-forged link rings true."
—KIPLING.

ONCE thoroughly awakened, the island-empire of Japan made rapid strides in civilisation. Perhaps Count Ito's speech in 1872 to his American brothers across the seas, sums up the condition of affairs best.

"To-day," he cries, "it is the earnest wish of our people to strive for the highest points of civilisation enjoyed by more enlightened countries. Looking to this end, we have adopted their military, naval, scientific, and educational institutions, and knowledge has flowed to us freely in the wake of foreign commerce. While held in absolute obedience by despotic sovereigns, through many thousand years, our people knew no freedom or liberty of thought. By educating our women we hope to ensure greater intelligence in future generations. Railways are being built, telegraph wires are stretching over many hundred miles of our territory, and nearly 1000 miles will be completed within a few months. Lighthouses now line our coasts, and our ship-yards are active. Japan is anxious to press forward." And then he adds, with a burst of enthusiasm: "The red disc in the centre of our national flag shall no longer appear like a wafer over a sealed empire, but henceforth the whole emblem of the Rising Sun, moving onward and upward amid the enlightened nations of the world."

Gradually European ways and customs crept into Japan; European dress was adopted by the Emperor and his officials. The capital, Tokyo, formerly known as Yedo, the Estuary Gate, was rebuilt; and though it has been devastated by fire and earthquake, typhoon and flood, yet, to-day, it is the national centre of the Japanese Empire, alive with new schemes and undertakings. It is lit with electric light, united by telephone and telegraph, and connected by railway with the port of Yokohama. Gay in spring with her masses of plum and cherry blossoms, she is the largest town in Asia, and seventh in the world.

In the year 1893, the armed strength of Japan was put to the test. "As the cherry flower is first among flowers, so should the warrior be first among men," the Japanese used to say.

The peninsula of the Korea, had long been a sort of shuttlecock between China and Japan. It was independent of either, but one day, rumours reached the court of Japan, that China was preparing for an invasion. Notwithstanding Japan's remonstrances, she continued her preparations. Then came a day, when a Chinese man-of-war fired at a Japanese battle-ship, and the long simmering discontent between the two countries broke into open war.

On September 17, 1894, a naval engagement took place, in which the Japanese ships were so smartly handled by the Japanese officers, that the Chinese were out-manœuvred at all points. From noon to sunset, the thunder of the great guns rolled over the waters of Korea Bay, "proclaiming to an amazed world the birth of a new Far East." After that fierce sea-fight, the Chinese ships escaped to Port Arthur: the sea-supremacy of Japan was established. Entering Manchuria, the Japanese land forces took the strong naval station of Port Arthur—to-day the terminus of the great Trans-Siberian railway. Then the port of Wei-hai-wei, 100 miles to the south-east, yielded to Japan, and the colossal empire of China was obliged to sue for peace to little Japan, one-fourth her size. She had thus swept the Chinese hordes from the Korea and Manchuria, driven the Chinese ships from the sea, and captured their two most important ports.

Every European country was loud in praise of Japanese methods, the discipline of Japanese men, the scientific warfare of Japanese officers, and the newly acquired patriotism of all.

An old Japanese lady, whose husband, brother, and sons had all been killed in the war, received the successive tidings with stoical calm, until the news came of the death of her youngest son, also in defence of his country. Then at last the poor mother burst into tears.

"I weep," she sobbed pathetically, "because I have no one left, whom I can send out to die for our country." This was patriotism worthy an older civilisation than that of Japan.

For men, who had never fought before, the courage of the young soldiers was splendid. A young Japanese bugler was standing by his captain at one of the battles, when a bullet struck him in the chest. Though knowing himself to be mortally wounded, he continued to blow his bugle, till his breath failed and he fell back dead.

The boy's father had the courage of his son. "It is the lot of all men to die," he cried. "My son had to die some time. His mother and I rejoice that our son has been loyal to Japan, even to shedding his blood in defence of her honour."

In the treaty that followed the war between Japan and China, the nations of Europe intervened. Russia obtained Port Arthur, for the terminus of her great Trans-Siberian railway, together with interests in Manchuria; Germany took the port of Kiao-chow, with interests in the Hoang-ho valley; while Britain occupied Wei-hai-wei, and insisted on full freedom of trade with China.

But perhaps the final stage in the recognition of Japan, as one of the nations of the world, was accomplished in 1902, when a treaty of alliance was signed between her and Great Britain, whose mutual policy was to stay the advancing growth of Russia and keep China for the Chinese.

CHAPTER 28

RUSSIA

"The peasant brain shall yet be wise,
  The untamed pulse grow calm and still;
 The blind shall see, the lowly rise
  And work in peace Time's wondrous will."

WHILE China was fighting against progress and Japan was hermetically sealed, the vast north of the Asiatic continent of Siberia was a little explored region, without communication with the outer world.

The growth of the Russian Empire is one of the most remarkable facts of modern history. We have already seen its first awakening under Peter the Great. In the dark cathedral at Petersburg, "amid surrendered keys and captured flags," sleeps that great king, whose monument is the Russian nation to-day.

"Peter was born and Russia was formed," Voltaire had once truly said. It would take too long to tell of the old hero Yermak, in the sixteenth century, who first crossed the Ural mountains, conquered the savage tribes in the desolate regions beyond, seized the capital Sibir, from which Siberia takes its name, and gave five million square miles to Russia in Asia. The wealth of fur, in this lonely region, drew on Russian explorers, at the same time that the Hudson's Bay Company were building forts in North America. The vast distances, the awful climate, the strange people, required heroism, of which these pioneers might justly be proud. Starvation and frost-bite took their yearly toll; more than once, it is recorded that men ate men in their extremity; but bravely they pushed on. Tobolsk was founded, the Lena river reached, the city of Yakutsk became a fur-trading centre, and at last the Russian flag was planted on the shores of the Pacific, at the Sea of Okhotsk. And "when the Russian flag has once been hoisted, it must never be lowered," said the Russians.

With the acquisition of Kamchatka, early in the eighteenth century, the Russian flag waved all over the northern territories of Asia, from the Ural Mountains to the sea. Only conflict with the Chinese Empire stopped further expansion for a time.

How Russia's efforts to obtain a "window towards Europe" were thwarted by England and France in the Crimea, has already been told. The story of the Afghan frontier is also told. Now we are concerned with Siberia, for, to-day, the story of Siberia is the story of Russia.

"Siberia is Russia," says a Russian traveller; "five million square miles, in which whole countries are a quivering carpet of wild-flowers in spring, a rolling grain-field in autumn, an ice-bound waste in winter, stored full of every mineral, crossed by the longest railway in the world, and largely inhabited by a population of convicts and exiles."

The exiles of Siberia conjure up a vision of all that is saddest in the world's history. The first exiles were Swedish prisoners of war sent to Kamchatka, after Pultowa, by Peter the Great, most of whom died before ever they reached their gloomy goal. Not only prisoners of war, but those accused of civil offences in Russia, were next banished, until masses of political offenders—for there is no freedom of thought in Russia—were exiled too.

Men, women, children, bound in chains, had to make their way on foot from Moscow to the Ural Mountains. At a famous boundary post, they bade farewell for ever to their native country, and stage by stage tramped wearily eastwards, begging their way from village to village. This was the refrain of their begging song:—

"For the sake of Christ
Have pity on us, oh our fathers."

Hundreds died before they reached the gloomy prison-houses of Tomsk and Irkutsk, which they should never leave again. There were scenes of terrible cruelty, and death was a welcome relief to the heart-broken exiles.

To-day such scenes are impossible. Exiles there still are and exiles there will be, until Russia's manhood awakens and demands freedom of thought.

Across the vast roadless country once trodden by long lines of hopeless exiles, runs the great iron railroad from Moscow to Port Arthur. The story of its growth is well known. Suggested by an Englishman, the scheme was laid before the Russian Government by enterprising Americans. In face of the changes coming over the Far East, it was decided to embark on the vast project. The present Tsar Nicholas laid the first stone of the railway himself in 1891, at Vladivostok—the "Lord of the East." For nearly 5000 miles, the iron road of "commerce and strategy" stretches eastwards from Europe to the shores of the Pacific. Nine days' travelling takes the passenger to Irkutsk, where the train is bodily lifted on to a steamer, specially constructed to break through the masses of ice and snow, which block Lake Baikal from December to April. This great Trans-Siberian railway—one of the greatest engineering feats of the age—forms the link to-day between Europe and Asia, between West and East, and who can foresee the infinite possibilities of the near future?

Such has been the development of Russia. Centuries of growth have given her an extent of territory superior to any other nation in the world. She is a nation among nations, and being a first-class military power, there is no reason she should not enlarge her boundaries further. She has long cast longing eyes towards India. Manchuria has not satisfied her designs on China.

But, turning to her internal life, we find that this great, this important country is living some centuries behind the rest of western Europe and America. Her Tsar is an autocratic ruler, and not one of her hundred and fifty million population has the slightest voice in her government. "Autocracy, orthodoxy, and militarism—these are the three pillars of the Russian State," says Tolstoi, a Russian social reformer. "We should all live according to the law of love, as the condition of bringing real brotherhood into a world torn by strife."

Tolstoi lives as he teaches others to live. Instead of ease and luxury, this man has chosen rather to live among the Russian peasants. With them he has ploughed the land and tilled the soil, with them he has reaped and sown: through the long winter, he has made boots, while he still teaches the law of love, the brotherhood of man.

It was in the spirit of Tolstoi that the Tsar summoned his great Peace Conference at the Hague in 1899. For a moment, men wondered if the vision of the poet might at last be realised:

> "The war-drum throbb'd no longer,
>   and the battle-flags were furl'd
>   In the Parliament of man,
>   the Federation of the world."

But the traditions of the past were too strong for Europe to accept such a condition then. It is this same tradition, that has prevented the Tsar of all the Russias from helping his country to throw off her old-world fetters. If the Poles have been forbidden their language, the Little Russians their literature, the Baltic Germans their religion, and the Finns their beloved constitution, it is because the government methods of the Tsar are not his own. They are the outcome of the soil and of the autocratic system of past generations, which he represents to-day—a system too strong for one man to fight, too old to be swept away at will, too deeply rooted for even a Tsar to cope with.

CHAPTER 29

THE ANNEXATION OF BURMA

"The Great Mother cometh over the sea."
—*Burmese Prophecy.*

WHEN Marco Polo visited China, he brought back news of two other great countries bordering on the land of the Great Khan—Tibet and Burma—both on the Indian frontier. Tibet lies dormant amid its snows, and plays no part at present in the world's history. But a different fate, fortunately, awaited Burma. A glance at the map will show that Burma occupies a remarkable geographical position. Bounded on three sides by India, China, and Siam, it has an unbroken coastline of some 800 miles, reaching to the Malay Peninsula. Running for over a thousand miles, throughout the whole length of the country, is the great waterway of the Irawadi, which rises in snowy Tibet and empties itself into the Bay of Bengal, its many mouths forming natural harbours of great commercial value. The country itself was rich in wealth: it produced rice for food, magnificent timber for building houses and ships, iron, coal, rubies, and precious stones. But the kings of Burma, with this magnificent empire at their feet, wastefully squandered the lives of the people and the treasure of the country in wars of aggression. Let us see how, after 2500 years of misgovernment, the "coming of the Great Queen" in 1885, brought peace and prosperity to a people of surpassing interest in themselves.

Early in the nineteenth century, the Burmese conquered Assam and first came into contact with British power in India, until in 1824, war broke out between the two powers. Knowing little of the country, British troops were landed at Rangoon in May, a few days before the rains, which, from May to October, converted the country into a gigantic swamp. The heavy rain fell incessantly day and night, fever broke out, and hundreds died. A campaign was carried on, until a stray cannon-ball killed the Burmese general, whose soldiers lost heart and allowed the enemy to sail up the Irawadi, almost to the walls of Ava, the old capital, near the present town of Mandalay. To save his capital, the king made peace, by which Assam and most of the west coast was ceded to the British.

Years passed on, but the Burmese were still unfriendly, and after a final protest, by the British, war broke out again. In 1852 British war-ships appeared at the mouth of the Irawadi, and troops made their way up the great river, capturing city after city, until Lower Burma was formally annexed to the British dominions in the Far East.

One of the chief features of this second Burmese war, was the capture of the famous golden Pagoda, or idol-temple, at Rangoon. This had been a goal for pilgrims for over 2000 years: they had come from Siam, Ceylon, the distant Shan hills, and even China, to worship at its numerous shrines. From a broad base, standing on a hill, rises the golden cupola of the Pagoda high into the sunny air to-day—the tapering point at the summit crowned by an umbrella, hung with golden bells set in jewels. Inside are beautifully carved roofs, glass mosaics, statues of Buddha, bronze bells, and precious stones, while crowds of worshippers are ever climbing the flights of steps north, south, east, and west. The capture of this by the British, brought home to the Burmese the fact, that their empire was slipping from them. They had no access to the sea now, save through the lost provinces in British hands.

A long peace followed. It was an era of prosperity for Lower Burma under Great Britain. The neglected land was cultivated, justice administered, and oppression relieved. Once, in 1855, a mission was sent to Calcutta begging for the restoration of the district; but the message from the English was decided. "So long as the sun shines in the heavens, so long will the British flag wave over Lower Burma."

With the accession of a new Burmese king, named Thebaw, in 1878, troubles once more broke out. His accession to the throne was signalised by a massacre of forty princes and princesses of royal descent. It is said that one of the royal princes met his death heroically. Turning to his brother, who was begging piteously for his life, he said: "My brother, it is not becoming to beg for life. We must die, for it is the custom. Had you been king, you would have given the same order. Let us die, since it is fated we must die."

The news of this cold-blooded massacre was received with horror throughout the civilised world.

"The King of Burma, being an independent sovereign, has a right to take all necessary measures to prevent disturbance in his dominion without the censure of others," said the Burmese minister.

King Thebaw, too, resented these criticisms. He insulted the British resident at Mandalay, and began to intrigue with the French, who, by the conquest of Tonquin, had extended their possessions to the borders of Upper Burma.

An incident known as the "Great Shoe Question" brought matters to a crisis. King Thebaw insisted that all Englishmen should take off their shoes on entering the royal palace. This they refused to do, and their position in Mandalay became so perilous, that they had to leave.

In the autumn of 1885, Thebaw issued a proclamation, calling on his subjects to join him, in driving the English into the sea. It was time for the British to take steps. General Prendergast, with 11,000 men, a fleet of flat-bottomed boats, and elephant batteries, received orders to invade Upper Burma.

"The Great White Queen is coming at last," said the Burmans, speaking of Queen Victoria, away in distant England. Still they took no steps to protect either their city or their king. The expedition advanced up the Irawadi.

> "On the road to Mandalay,
> Where the old Flotilla lay,
> Can't you hear their paddles chunkin'
> from Rangoon to Mandalay?"

They reached the royal city with little opposition. The king and his queen had retired to a summer-house in the palace gardens to await the British, with whom they intended to make peace. To distract their minds, the maidens of the Burmese court were dancing, while near at hand stood the royal elephants, laden with treasure and ready for flight.

To the royal palace marched the British, to demand the surrender of the Burmese king and his kingdom within twenty-four hours. The blow had fallen at last. It was too late to think of escape.

Early next morning King Thebaw was hurried into a bullock-cart with little ceremony, his queen into another, and in the presence of a great crowd of weeping and awestruck subjects, they were conveyed to a steamer on the Irawadi. Here a guard of British soldiers was drawn up: they presented arms on the appearance of the royal prisoners. As their bayonets flashed in the sunlight, the king fell on his knees in abject terror.

"They will kill me," he cried wildly. "Save my life."

His queen was braver. She strode on erect— her little child clinging to her dress—fierce and dauntless to the last. So the king and queen of Burma were exiled to Ceylon, where they still live. The great country of Burma was conquered afterwards, but it was some years before it quieted down.

Administered by British officials, the country was then restored to a state of prosperity. Trade increased rapidly, a railway was made from Rangoon to Mandalay, telegraph wires were laid, and with all this, Burmese customs were respected. The great feature of the country is still its pagodas. Still every little village shows its cluster of white cupolas, while the golden umbrellas, which surmount the glistening pinnacles, flash under the fierce Eastern sun. The building of these pagodas, in memory of the great teacher Buddha, is an act of merit among the devout Burmans. Their worship of Buddha is at once real and true. It moulds their view of life, gives motives to their endeavours, and "reveals the Great Hereafter." Their heaven, or Nirvana, is only attained by self-denial and self-sacrifice: to gain Eternal Peace is more to them than the possession of this world's goods.

"The thoughts of his heart, these are the wealth of a man," they affirm with confidence. So life and death are filled with the one great hope, that at the last, each faithful Burman shall enter into the "Great Peace."

CHAPTER 30

THE STORY OF AFGHANISTAN

"Quoth he: 'Of the Russians, who can say?
    When the night is gathering, all is grey;
    But we look that the gloom of the night shall die
    In the morning flush of a blood-red sky.' "
                                            —KIPLING.

IF the Burmese had proved troublesome neighbours on the eastern frontier of India, yet more tiresome neighbours dwelt on the other side of the north-west boundary. Here lies the great region of Afghanistan, guarded by the gigantic range of the Hindu Kush— the highway between Persia and India, and, yet more important, the highway between Russia and the British dominions in India.

Early in the nineteenth century, the ruler or Amir of Afghanistan, made an alliance with Russia. This alliance was regarded with alarm by the British, as Russia had long threatened an advance on India, the road to which land would now lie open. So in January 1839, a large British and Indian army crossed the Indus, advanced unopposed through the Bolan Pass to the fortress of Quetta, took possession of Kandahar, fought their way through Ghazni, took

Jelalabad, and entered Kabul. Dost Mahomed fled from the capital with a few horsemen to the mountains of the Hindu Kush, and an exiled Afghan prince was proclaimed Amir in his stead. The conquest of the country was considered complete, but the English had altogether mistaken the character of the Afghans. Small rebellions, headed by Akbar Khan, a son of Dost Mahomed, took place. The British Resident, Sir William Macnaghten, was warned of coming danger, which he disregarded, till one day he learned the horrible news, that two English officials had been surrounded and butchered in cold blood by Afghans. A few weeks later, he agreed to meet Akbar Khan at a conference on the banks of a neighbouring river near Kabul, to discuss plans. The conference had hardly begun, when the Amir drew from his belt a pair of pistols, which Macnaghten had given him, and shot the unfortunate Englishman dead. After such treachery, the only safety for the British garrison at Kabul lay in retreat. Akbar Khan promised to protect the army, if it would return at once to India.

On January 6, 1842, the troops left the Afghan capital. It was the heart of a cruel winter. Snow and ice lay thickly on the great passes of Khurd Kabul and Kyber, which had to be climbed before the plains of India could be reached. The first of these was a terrible gorge, running some five miles between mountain-ranges, narrow, high, and dark, with a mountain-torrent rushing fiercely down from the hills. As men, women, and children made their way along this snowy pass, crowds of savage

Afghans from the rocks above, shot them down one by one. In hopeless confusion, they staggered on; Akbar took pity on the women and children, and put them in a safe place till the fury of his people should be past. On pushed the soldiers. After five days' march, out of the 14,500 men, who had left Kabul, only 4000 remained. Each day the massacre was resumed. At last only sixty-five were left out of the mighty host that had started. These forced their way on towards Jelalabad, which was held by an English garrison. One man alone survived. Weary and fainting from exhaustion, Dr Brydon staggered into the city, to tell the tale of one of the most awful catastrophes in the history of mankind. The disaster was retrieved later, by another advance on Kabul, which ended in the rout of Akbar Khan.

Time passed on. Another of Dost Mahomed's sons succeeded to the Afghan throne—Shere Ali Khan—who was no more friendly to the English than his brother had been. When relations between Russia and England were sorely strained, he received and welcomed a Russian mission at Kabul, refusing the British demand for a like concession.

Negotiations ended in war. Once more British troops marched by Jelalabad and Kandahar to Kabul. Shere Ali fled from his capital, his son, Yakub Khan, was proclaimed Amir, and a treaty of peace was signed, by which the Amir agreed to allow an Englishman to reside at Kabul. In 1879, the British resident arrived and took up his abode in the Residency at Kabul. Suddenly the news fell like a thunderbolt, that the terrible tragedies of former years had been repeated. The English in Kabul had been attacked, and after gallant resistance, had been cut to pieces by the Afghans.

Yet once again British troops, under Lord Roberts, marched to the Afghan capital. Yakub Khan surrendered and was exiled to India, while Abdur Rahman, the eldest grandson of Dost Mahomed, was proclaimed Amir. A good soldier and a good statesman was Abdur Rahman, who ruled his country for the next twenty years, but the early part of his reign was clouded by the rising of his cousin, who wished to be Amir. In the summer of 1880, this dangerous rival marched towards Kandahar with a large following of Afghan cavalry, and on July 27, one of the most grievous disasters in the history of the British army took place at Maiwand, when an English brigade was annihilated by the new pretender to the throne. This is the story. To stop the advancing Afghan army, General Burrows had marched forth with British troops towards Maiwand, on the Helmond river, when suddenly the whole Afghan army charged down on the little force. The British blunder was redeemed by magnificent heroism, and there is no finer record in history than that of the famous Sixty-sixth, or Royal Berkshire Regiment, rallying again and again in the face of overwhelming odds, till at the last the soldiers formed a square, and fighting back to back, died to a man.

To redeem British prestige and suppress the victorious rival, Lord Roberts now made his historic march from Kabul to Kandahar, to relieve the hard-pressed garrison there. It was a distance of 300 miles, haunted by bands of hostile Afghans, who might attack them at any moment. But Lord Roberts was equal to the task. After twenty days of hard marching he brought his 10,000 men safe to Kandahar, where he soon put Ayub Khan to flight and saved a difficult situation. From this time Abdur Rahman reigned over his difficult country in peace and friendship with the British in India, till in 1901 he died and was succeeded by his eldest son Habibullah as Amir of Afghanistan.

CHAPTER 31

THE EMPIRE OF INDIA

"Are there thunders moaning in the distance?
Are there spectres moving in the darkness?
Trust the Hand of Light will lead her people,
Till the thunders pass, the spectres vanish,
And the Light is Victor and the darkness
Dawns into the Jubilee of the Ages."
—TENNYSON.

THE stories of Burma and Afghanistan—the two
countries bordering on India—have been told. Let
us take a last look at the India of to-day, and gather
up the threads of this great British dependency,
which in 1903 celebrated the accession of her British
Emperor with such enthusiasm. Through the dark
days of the Indian mutiny, England had saved India
from herself. With the death of the East India
Company, a Royal Proclamation announced that the
Queen of England had assumed the government of
British territory in India. A new era opened for the
country—an era of religious toleration, of
development, and progress under the British flag.
With the opening of the Suez Canal, constructed by
the genius of a French engineer in 1869, India was

184

brought into closer communication with England. It was through this Suez Canal, that the present King of England visited India in 1875. A warm welcome awaited the "Son of the Great Queen beyond the seas." The visit was rich in results.

On January 1, 1877, a magnificent Durbar, or state reception, was held at Delhi, the old Mogul capital, at which the "Queen beyond the seas" was proclaimed "Empress of India." Nothing could exceed the splendour of native chiefs and rulers who attended: no such gorgeous assembly had ever gathered in India before. And the sun shone down on the brilliantly coloured costumes, till the grounds looked like "an immense Eastern garden in full bloom." Each chief came on his own royal elephant, which was arrayed in gorgeous trappings with a throne of gold on its back. To each was presented a golden banner and a medal bearing the new legend, "Victoria, Empress." Out of compliment to these loyal princes, the English Viceroy, the Queen's representative, came on the state elephant, kept for great occasions. To the strains of the National Anthem, he then took his seat on the throne, twelve heralds sounded a flourish of trumpets, and the Proclamation was read aloud.

"The strong hand of Imperial power is put forth, not to crush but to protect and guide; and the results of British rule are everywhere around us, in rapid advance of the whole country and the increasing prosperity of all its provinces.

"God save the Queen of the United Kingdom and Empress of India."

This was the final scene in the establishment of the British Empire in India. During the rise and growth of British power, the Mogul Empire had faded away. If fleeting memories of its past splendour flickered in Oriental imagination, they have long since died out in the hearts of the people. Old feuds were forgotten, new friendships were formed. Loyalty had been slow in growing, but as time rolls on, it becomes deeper rooted and wider spread—loyalty to that queen and country which, for 100 years, had ever tried to deal out even-handed justice to all alike.

Meanwhile dark clouds were gathering on the north-west frontier. Chitral was a small mountain state bordering on Kashmir, hidden away amid the snowy ranges of the Hindu Kush. An English resident resided here, to protect British interests. When troubles broke out in 1895, he was driven into a fort with his attendants, and there besieged by the turbulent tribesmen of the country.

Expeditions were immediately despatched to his relief. The famous race for Chitral, fills one of the most thrilling pages of modern history.

While a large force under Sir Robert Low fought its way over the Malakand Pass, Colonel Kelly, with some 400 men, was making his way from Gilgit on the frontier, over a yet higher pass, covered with four feet of soft snow.

It would take too long to tell how this little band of pioneers climbed the snowy mountain-passes, while snow fell heavily from the pitiless sky; how man after man was struck with snow-blindness, man after man was frost-bitten with the stinging cold. Such courage has its reward. After a fortnight's struggle, Kelly reached Chitral to find that the home-made Union-jack still waved over the fort, which had been held by its gallant defenders for forty-six days. Peace was soon restored, and to-day Chitral is the most advanced northern post in India.

Meanwhile trouble was brewing farther south on the Punjab frontier. In 1897, Sir William Lockhart led an expedition from Peshawur to Tirah, the headquarters of a tribe known as Afridis, who had attacked British outposts in the Kyber Pass. Again the advance lay through a difficult mountainous district, where tribesmen on the heights commanded the passes. Severe fighting took place at Dargai, which was strongly defended by the enemy. The British advance was led by native Gurkhas, who climbed up a zigzag path under a perpendicular cliff swept by the enemy's fire. But with all their courage, they could not carry the post, and the Gordon Highlanders were brought to the front.

"Men," cried their Colonel, "the position must be taken at all costs. The Gordon Highlanders will take it."

With fixed bayonets, the Highlanders made one of their famous charges, mounted the heights and carried all before them. The story of the Highland piper, who, though shot through both his ankles, sat on the ground and continued piping, will not easily be forgotten by those who love to hear of heroic deeds.

Having taken Dargai, the expedition marched on to Tirah, but eventually, after hard fighting, peace was restored to the north-west frontier.

Since these days the frontier has been strengthened against all possible invasion, and a line of forts and fortified posts protect the passes into Indian territory.

There is one more scene to describe before we take leave of India. Magnificent as was the Delhi Durbar of 1877, yet perhaps more gorgeous still was the Durbar that met on January 1, 1903, to proclaim the accession of Edward VII. to the Imperial throne of India. Everything was on a gigantic scale. Elephants, with gold and silver howdahs flashing with gems, bore some hundred Indian princes of rank to the old Mogul capital to do honour to the new sovereign. As the sun lit up the brilliant scene, the blazing gorgeousness of the East mixed strangely with the more regulated splendour of the West. The king's brother was with the Viceroy, Lord Curzon, whose speech summed up the advance of twenty-six years.

"To the majority of these millions," he said, addressing the vast multitude before him, "the king's government has given freedom from invasion; to others, it has guaranteed their rights and privileges;

to others, it opens ever-widening avenues of honourable employment; to the masses, it dispenses mercy in the hour of suffering; to all, it endeavours to give equal justice, immunity from oppression, and the blessing of peace. To have won such a kingdom is a great achievement; to hold it by fair and righteous dealing is a greater; to weld it by prudent statesmanship into a single and compact whole, will be and is the greatest of all."

Such is—

> "The Ocean-empire, with her boundless homes
> For ever broadening England and her throne
> In the vast Orient."

CHAPTER 32

GORDON—THE HERO OF KHARTUM

"Warrior of God, man's friend, not here below
But somewhere dead far in the waste Sudan,
Thou livest in all hearts, for all men know
This earth hath borne no simpler, nobler man."
—TENNYSON.

ON his way to India, to attend the Coronation Durbar, the Duke of Connaught had stopped in Egypt, to be present at the opening of the famous Asuan dam, which has so benefited the dwellers by the mighty Nile. Let us glance at Egypt for a moment.

Egypt was governed by one Ismail, a Khedive or Sovereign, who ruled the country subject to the Sultan of Turkey. The opening of the Suez Canal, connecting the Mediterranean Sea with the Red Sea, in 1869, drew the eyes of Europe to this old country of the Pharaohs, which was being sorely misgoverned by Ismail. Indeed, so reckless and extravagant was his expenditure, that Egypt was threatened with ruin, and it became necessary for European powers to interfere with the Government.

To make a long story short, Ismail was finally deposed in 1879, his eldest son Tewfik was made Khedive, and England and France jointly assumed the task of controlling the new Government. But this interference was resented by Arabi the Egyptian, under whom a rebellion now broke out. Force became necessary. A British fleet bombarded the forts defending Alexandria, which had been strongly fortified by Arabi. From dawn to sunset, through the hot hours of that July day, the great English guns boomed over the city. The forts were silenced, but for two nights and a day, the European inhabitants were exposed to the fury of Arabi's soldiers, and part of the city was burned to the ground. Two months later, the British army under Sir Garnet Wolseley, who had so successfully led the expedition in Canada against Louis Riel, defeated the Egyptians at Tel-el-Kebir, and with "one brilliant dash scattered to the winds the hopes and forces" of Arabi. Next day, the British cavalry rode in hot haste across the thirty miles of scorching desert to Cairo, where Arabi surrendered himself with 10,000 Egyptians. The Khedive's authority was thus restored, and Arabi was transported to Ceylon. England was now obliged to assume the protectorate of Egypt, to assure the future progress of the country in which, by reason of the Suez Canal, she had so much interest. She helped the Khedive to improve the condition of his wretched people, to replace injustice and oppression by justice and mercy.

"It is by such action, that the British nation realises its Imperial ideal of duty."

Meanwhile in the Sudan, a Mohammedan fanatic, calling himself the Mandi, roused his Mohammedan followers against the Government, which extended over the Sudan beyond Khartum at the junction of the Blue and White Niles. Preparations were made in Cairo at once to crush the rebellion. A force of 10,000 men was hurriedly collected. Unwilling recruits were forced into the ranks, Egyptian peasants were taken from the fields, the very donkey-boys of Cairo were armed to swell this unwieldy rabble army, which was placed under the command of Colonel Hicks. But the Egyptian Government little realised the size and strength of the rebel army awaiting their prey in the solitude of the vast desert. Hicks Pasha and his 10,000 men went bravely forth to "dare the impossible," and were never seen again. With the complete destruction of the army, consternation fell upon Cairo. The Khedive's power over the Sudan seemed at an end, and it was at last decided to withdraw from this desert land in the south altogether. Still there were isolated European garrisons in distant provinces: there was loyal Khartum itself, and from these arose a cry for help, which reached the ears of one Englishman—the heroic and enthusiastic Gordon.

"Chinese Gordon" had already spent years in the Sudan. On the death of Livingstone, he had been made Governor-General of the Sudan, for the suppression of the slave trade. He loved the black men of the Sudan, and now, in hopes of saving the loyal garrison at Khartum, he left England for Cairo. It was January 24, 1884, when he arrived. Two days later, a few faithful friends bid farewell to him and his one companion, Colonel Stewart, little thinking, as the train rolled away into the night, that they had looked their last on the two cheerful determined faces of the men, who were giving their lives to a "task of mercy beyond human strength."

That day year, Gordon stood face to face with death, away in lonely Khartum. To the panic-stricken garrison, Gordon had sent a telegram—"Be not afraid, I am coming." Arrived at Korosko, he plunged into the silent desert on his camel: every moment was precious. Never did man ride on so urgent and desperate an undertaking before. At last he arrived at Khartum. As he entered his capital, people crowded enthusiastically about him, kissing his hands, and greeting him as the saviour of the Sudan.

"I come without soldiers, but with God on my side, to redress the evils of this land," he cried to his faithful blacks; "I will not fight with any weapons save justice."

But the times were more anxious than even Gordon recognised. Daily, the rebel force was growing in strength. Within a fortnight, telegraphic communication between the little white city in the burning desert and Cairo was cut off. By April, Khartum was closely invested by the Mandi's troops. The whole of the Sudan, except Khartum and the

Red Sea ports, were in the hands of the Mandi. For the next five months, a great silence fell over the little desert city, within which, two brave men were busy strengthening their defences and cheering the little garrison. The Nile rose and fell. In September, Gordon despatched a steamer under Colonel Stewart, to make its way to Cairo for help. But the little "Abbas" never reached its destination. Colonel Stewart was treacherously killed near Abu Hamed, and the silence between Cairo and Khartum remained unbroken.

Gordon was now alone—the only Englishman in that far-off desert city. His last pathetic journals describe his days during those long sad weeks. Busy all day in defending the town and ministering to the wants of his people, every night he mounted to the palace roof, and there, "alone with his duty and his God," he kept his long lonely watch over the ramparts, praying for the help that never came. A relief expedition under Lord Wolseley had already started, and Gordon always felt there was the possibility that one day, "after the golden after-glow or in the solemn whitening of the dawn," his watchful eye might detect a cloud of dust, a movement of shadows, or the sudden flash of a bayonet, to show he had not been forgotten, that help was coming and the dreary siege should end.

An expedition was indeed struggling forwards to his relief. The British forces under Wolseley, helped by Canadian boatmen, were pushing on by river and desert.

Gordon's lonely watch over the ramparts.

Sunday, January 25, arrived. While the city slept, the Mandi's men, known as dervishes, were creeping towards the parapets of Khartum. The moon had gone down: the night was dark. There was little enough to impede their progress: only a few starving soldiers looked wearily over the parapet. With yells and screams, the dervishes rushed upon the sleeping people. In a surging mass, they threw themselves on to the palace, where Gordon kept watch. And just as the red sun was rising over the dark horizon, they killed him, cut off his head, and carried it to the Mandi in triumph. Two days later— it was Gordon's birthday—a few Englishmen from the relief expedition pushed their way to Khartum, to find they were too late. A massacre of the garrison had taken place, and the man they had come to save, had fallen at his post of duty—faithful unto death.

"By those for whom he lived, he died. His land
  Awoke too late, and crowned dead brows with praise.
He, 'neath the blue that burns o'er Libyan sand,
  Put off the burden of heroic days."

The Mandi had established his kingdom from Egypt to the Bahr-el-Ghazal, from Darfur to the Red Sea, and the British withdrew to Wady Halfa on the Nile—for a time.

CHAPTER 33

THE REDEMPTION OF EGYPT

"Heart of England, faltering never in the good time or the ill,
But thy great day's task of duty strong and patient to fulfil."
—TRENCH.

THE abandonment of the Sudan had a disastrous effect on the situation in Egypt, where one of England's greatest statesmen, Lord Cromer, strove patiently with the apparently hopeless position. Through the storm and stress of those dark days, he emerged triumphantly at last—the redeemer of a new Egypt. By his thorough and far-reaching reforms, he raised the whole country, from a state bordering on ruin, to that of prosperity, peace, and happiness. If one great need cried out above the rest, it was the want of proper irrigation or artificial watering of the land.

The story of the annual overflow of the Nile, from the days of Joseph, has already been told. A system of irrigation had existed through long ages, but owing to the extravagance of Ismail, the canals and dams had fallen into neglect and disuse, while the delta of the Nile, the old land of Goshen—the granary of the ancient world—was a hopeless swamp.

With the courage of a far-seeing administrator, Lord Cromer set to work on the skilful irrigation of Egypt without delay. Notwithstanding the huge debt on the country, he boldly borrowed an extra million pounds, to reclaim the country. The land was divided into five circles and placed under Anglo-Indian engineers of skill and experience, who worked with a will at a new system of drainage and irrigation. For long years they worked with a single-hearted devotion at their difficult task, with wonderful results. Whole new districts were brought under cultivation, and the wealth of the land increased by leaps and bounds. Here is a story showing how necessary was this work to the Egyptians. The year 1888 was a very low Nile, and a large area of country was threatened with failure of water. The canal feeding the district was too low to spread the water over the thirsty fields.

In their despair the people turned to the Inspector of the district. He saw that a dam must be thrown across the canal, in order to raise the water to the required level. Gladly the Egyptians worked under their English friend, who brought his bed to the canal bank, never leaving the scene of action till the work was finished. It was completely successful: the fields were flooded, the district was saved, and the Egyptians could not be grateful enough to their deliverer.

Meanwhile the famous dam or Barrage in the Nile delta was being restored by Sir Colin Scott Moncrieff. It had been built by a French engineer: at vast trouble and expense he had thrown sixty-one arches over the Rosetta branch of the Nile mouth and sixty-one over the Damietta branch. Now the timbers were rotten, the iron rusty, and it took years of work by night and day, to set it going again.

"It is like mending a watch and never stopping the works," said Sir Colin. But he carried through the work, and soon the produce of the fertile delta land was doubled.

Perhaps the reform that added most to the progress of the world was the reform of the army. It was the same old story over again—"Egyptian hands and English heads." The Egyptians were officered and drilled by Englishmen, until they became efficient soldiers, who can now do and dare what in former days was the impossible. It was partly with these men that Lord Kitchener won the battle of Omdurman, with these men he conquered the Sudan and destroyed the Khalifa's power. Let us tell the story of his expedition.

The Mandi died soon after the fall of Khartum, leaving his great territories to the Khalifa, or Commander-in-Chief. The Khalifa at once built an immense tomb over the Mandi's body at Omdurman—a village opposite the ruins of Khartum, at the junction of the Blue and White Niles. He had compelled every man in his vast dominion to serve in his armies, so that no crops were sown: food was scarce, and famine and disease spread through the length and depth of the Sudan.

There was no doubt that Egypt and England, side by side, must reclaim and reconquer this unhappy land of the blacks. This difficult task was entrusted to Lord Kitchener, Sirdar or Commander-in-Chief of the Egyptian army. For four years preparations had been going quietly forward between Cairo and Wady Haifa, till in March 1896, the world was startled by the news that he had started on an expedition to Dongola. All was in readiness. Here, at Wady Haifa, had been forged the deadliest weapon that was ever waged against Mahdism—the Sudan railway, which even now extended some way beyond the frontier.

"The battle of Omdurman was won in the work-shops of Wady Haifa," said an eyewitness of the whole campaign.

Be this as it may, the launching of rails and sleepers into the vast desert, when the far end of the line was yet in the hands of the enemy, was one of the bravest acts in history, and it was due to the dauntless courage and fierce determination of the Sirdar and his clever engineer.

The telegraph followed the railway: the wires, in lengths of a mile, being coiled on revolving wheels and carried on camels. Thus, accompanied by rail and telegraph, the great expedition pressed forward into the burning desert. It would take too long to tell, of how the army toiled onward by rail and river, now carrying their transport round the great cataracts on the backs of camels, now navigating the shallow reaches of the river in light sailing craft, now marching across desert tracts with the scorching sun shining pitilessly down upon them, now impeded by terrific sand-storms, till fever broke out in their midst.

At last they reached Dongola, which was captured from the Khalifa after severe fighting, and the Khedive's flag floated once more over a long-lost province. By the end of the year, the railway had reached Dongola. The Sirdar now busied himself over a new line, which should cut right across the waterless Nubian desert, encircled by the wide western sweep of the Nile from Wady Haifa to Abu Hamed, where the river bends again southwards to Khartum. By July 1897, such progress had been made, that an Egyptian force advanced rapidly by the Nile to Abu Hamed, and wrested that post from the Khalifa's garrison. The blow was so sudden and unexpected, that the dervishes now abandoned Berber, 150 miles to the south, near the junction of the Atbara and Nile.

The time was now ripe for the general advance: the end was already in sight. On Good Friday, April 8, 1898, a brilliant and crushing victory was won by Egyptian and English troops at the Atbara, where some 16,000 dervishes lay entrenched in a zariba.

The Khalifa now rallied his fanatical host for the last time, for the defence of his capital, on the plains of Omdurman. The Sirdar led 22,000 men against him. As the great army advanced, nothing was visible, but the big white dome of the Mahdi's tomb gleaming through the desert haze. Early in the morning of September 2, shouts of the advancing host were heard, and in a vast mass, the Khalifa's black army with waving flags moved forward across the desert, to attack the Sirdar's host of Anglo-Egyptians. Fearlessly the fanatics moved forward, spears in hand, but they could not withstand the firearms of civilisation. For four hours the battle raged, which was to decide the fate of the Sudan. Then the dervishes fled from the slaughter. The Khalifa's body-guard had fallen to a man around the black flag, but their master had fled.

The Sirdar then pushed on to Omdurman. Riding coolly into the town, still held by some 5000 dervishes, he offered to spare their lives, if they would surrender. This piece of cool daring overawed them. His life was in their hands for the moment, but they knew the army was behind, their cause was lost, and they laid down their arms. So Omdurman, the Khalifa's last stronghold, was captured.

A touching incident followed. The following Sunday, the troops formed up in the open space facing the ruined palace of Khartum, where Gordon, thirteen years before, had laid down his life. On the very roof, from which he had watched so long and anxiously, the flags of Egypt and England flew side by side in the blazing sunshine. Gordon's work had been finished at last. The restless Sudan belonged to Egypt, and the Khedive, with England's help, had restored peace and freedom to one of the most oppressed nations of the earth.

A new Khartum soon arose amid the ruins of the old town. In the midst of it arises the Gordon College, built in memory of its brave defender, for the education of the Sudanese. Here, too, is the capital of the Sudan administration, carried on by a Governor-General, with telegraphic communication to every province, and a good railway service to Cairo.

Thus every year does Egypt become more civilised, and more prosperous, and better fitted to take her place among the great nations of the world.

CHAPTER 34

THE STORY OF BRITISH WEST AFRICA

"Clear the land of evil, drive the road and bridge the ford."
—KIPLING.

THE occupation of Khartum was followed by a strange incident. Some 400 miles to the south, Lord Kitchener found the French flag flying from the desert city of Fashoda. Captain Marchand, on behalf of the French Government, had overstepped the bounds of the French Sudan, and he was obliged reluctantly to retire, through Egyptian territory, to France.

The French were already the largest land-owners in West Africa—their possessions stretching from Lake Chad to Cape Verd, from Algeria to the Gulf of Guinea. Of late years, notwithstanding the energy of modern French colonisation, the British Empire has expanded yet more rapidly in this quarter, and territories, hitherto vast tracts considered as barren wastes of drifting sand, have been included in the British sphere of influence.

The west coast of Africa calls up a vision of old Hanno, the Carthaginian, seeking colonies for the Old World: then falls a silence of twenty centuries, broken by the Portuguese sailing from point to point, urged on by the enthusiasm of Prince Henry. Europeans followed, bringing back gold-dust and negro slaves, until this coast of Guinea was literally studded with forts and factories for purposes of trade.

A curious story is connected with this name. One day, some early European traders asked the black natives where they got the gold, which they offered for sale on the coast.

"From Jenne," they replied, naming an inland town on the banks of the Niger.

So the name was given to the coast of Guinea, and indirectly to a British coin, struck from the first piece of gold that came from here.

Low-lying and unhealthy is this West African coast, upon which great Atlantic rollers thunder unceasingly, fringing the shore with boiling surf, which makes landing difficult and dangerous. Inland, is a thickly wooded and well-watered land, with an unlimited wealth of gold and a deadly climate for Europeans.

Nevertheless many Europeans live there, and a glance at the map will show, how quaintly their colonies are wedged in together. The mouth of the Senegal river is French, the mouth of the Gambia is English. Portuguese and French Guinea divide Gambia from her sister colony of Sierra Leone, some 500 miles by sea; the negro republic of Liberia and the French Ivory Coast, divide Sierra Leone from the third English possession, the Gold Coast, 800 miles away, which is separated by German and French territory 300 miles in length, from Lagos and Nigeria.

It would take too long to tell the story of each of these English Crown Colonies—Gambia, Sierra Leone, the Gold Coast, Lagos, and Nigeria. Sierra Leone, or the Mountains of the Lion, has been called the "White Man's Grave"; but indeed the whole of this coast is fever-stricken, and many a white man has gone, never to return from this beautiful and deadly region. Perhaps the majority have perished in the Gold Coast, where in 1874 the presence of British soldiers was necessary to put down the warrior tribe of Ashantis, who occupied the hinterland and resented the white men's possession of the Gold Coast. After many attempts in past years to drive out the English, the whole Ashanti army marched to the invasion of the colony, under their great black King Koffee.

"I will carry my golden stool to Cape Coast Castle, and there wash it in English blood," said the King of the Ashantis.

The guns at Cape Coast Castle saved the town, but it was necessary to take some severe measures, if the colony were to be saved from these savage warriors. So Sir Garnet Wolseley, the leader of the Red River expedition in Canada, was sent to suppress the Ashantis, with British and West Indian troops. Early in the year 1874, a start was made from the camp at Prahsu, some seventy miles from the coast, for the hundred miles to Kumassi, the capital of the Ashanti kingdom. They had to march through a dense tropical forest, its huge trees matted together with creepers, through which no sun could penetrate, no breeze could cool the stifling atmosphere. Only the chatter of monkeys and the flutter of bright-plumed birds broke the deep silence. The troops pressed laboriously forward. Meanwhile the Ashantis had taken up a position on a commanding height twenty miles from Kumassi, with every prospect of success. They outnumbered the foe by five to one; they were surrounded by impenetrable bush; they had never known defeat.

On January 31, the battle began. For some hours the position was shelled by British guns and rockets, and the position finally carried by the Highlanders, who swept forwards, with their bagpipes playing the while. Then the whole Ashanti army turned and fled in the wildest disorder towards Kumassi. The ground was strewn with traces of their flight: umbrellas, drums, muskets, and dying men strewed the line of their retreat. The king himself, who had watched the battle seated on his golden stool, under a red umbrella, fled with the rest. They were pursued by the British to Kumassi. In vain did the black men offer human sacrifices, after their ignorant custom: the king had disappeared, and nothing remained but to set on fire his savage capital and make peace. The campaign had been a brilliant success, and for the moment it seemed as if Ashanti power were at an end. But it was not so. Kumassi was soon rebuilt; a new king, Prempeh, inherited the golden stool or throne of Ashanti, and continued human sacrifices, interfered with British trade, and failed to carry out the terms of the treaty. Once more, in 1896, a British army advanced to Kumassi, but this time the Ashantis refused to fight. The troops entered the capital with the Union-jack flying, took King Prempeh prisoner, and annexed the kingdom of Ashanti to the Gold Coast Colony.

But the latest addition to the West African colonies is Nigeria, the land watered by the mighty Niger, explored in the eighteenth century by Mungo Park. Two men, Denham and Clapperton, had taken up his incomplete work. Crossing the great desert from Tripoli, they struck the Niger, wandered over the Houssa States and the shores of Lake Chad, reached Sokoto, and drew aside the veil of the French Sudan for the first time. Clapperton died of fever at Sokoto, and his servant, Richard Lander, undertook to carry on his work. After many adventures, he reached the mouth of the Niger in 1830, and the thunder of the surf upon the shore convinced him, that the mystery of the Niger was solved at last. The Niger was mostly discovered by British enterprise, but its possession by England to-day is due largely to one—Sir George Goldie. He gave to his country Nigeria, a tract of land four times the size of the British Isles, just as Cecil Rhodes gave her Rhodesia.

Goldie had travelled much in the country: he had seen the tyranny of the slave trade, the barbarism of the natives, the terrors of human sacrifices, and he knew that England must reclaim and administer this unhappy country of the blacks. Here is the story of one district. Benin City stood on the river Benin, which flows into the Bight of Benin, a veritable death-trap.

"Beware and take care of the Bight of Benin,
　Whence few come out though many go in,"

sang the sailors of olden times.

Now the abolition of the slave trade had infuriated the cruel king of Benin, who swore eternal hatred to all Europeans and closed his door to their trade. In the year 1897, an English mission started for Benin City, to try and induce the king to open his country to their traders; but before ever they reached the city a shot rang through the air, and all save two were massacred in cold blood by orders of the king. A punitive expedition followed this treachery, and Englishmen made their way to the city to find a condition of affairs that defies description; in every direction they found crucified bodies, the remains of human sacrifices, heads and skulls. There was nothing to do, but to set fire to this City of Blood, from which the king had already fled. It was time for this country to be placed under some civilised state, and in 1900 England announced her protectorate over Nigeria.

To that country she has brought civilisation and progress, peace and, justice, carrying out those principles, which alone justify annexation.

CHAPTER 35

THE STORY OF UGANDA

"Lead us and teach us, till earth and heaven
Grow larger around us and higher above."
—MRS BROWNING.

LONG before the conquest of the Egyptian Sudan, men had been exploring the land to the south, in order to discover the sources of the Nile. The story of how Bruce discovered the source of the Blue Nile has already been told. Men of all nations had vied with one another in their search for the sources of the White Nile, which flows past Omdurman and Fashoda. Even a lady, "the richest heiress in the Netherlands," started with her mother and aunt, her lady's-maid and 200 servants, to explore a tributary of the White Nile, the Bahr-el-Ghazal. But the country is unhealthy for Europeans. Her mother and aunt died of fever, and she herself was subsequently murdered by natives.

It was reserved for Englishmen to make the final discovery. While Livingstone was exploring the Nyassa region, two explorers were leaving Zanzibar to investigate a large lake, known to lie north of

Tanganyika. Disaster dogged their steps through this fever-stricken country, guides deserted them, illness assailed them; but with that resolute perseverance, which alone ensures success, they pushed on towards their goal. But one of them—Grant—soon grew too ill to go farther, and it was left for his more fortunate companion, Speke, to behold the great sheet of water, to which he gave the name of Victoria Nyanza or Victoria Lake, after his queen. He discovered that the Nile flowed out of this great lake to the northward, though he missed the lake into which it next flowed. This discovery was left to another Englishman, Baker, who with his wife met Speke on his way to Khartum. After learning Speke's great news they journeyed on, to be rewarded by finding a lesser lake to the west of Victoria Nyanza, which they at once christened Albert Nyanza, after Prince Albert, the husband of the Queen of England, who had recently died. Into this lake they traced the Nile's entrance and exit, and with this great news they made their way homewards.

Their way was terribly impeded by thick tangles of a water-weed, known as the sudd, which choked the upper reaches of the Nile. To-day the sudd has been removed at great labour and expense, and the river thus rendered navigable as far as Gondokoro.

Much light had been thrown on this country beyond the Sudan, but still the geography was uncertain, when Stanley, in 1875, closed the quest of 2000 years for the source of the Nile. His intercourse with Livingstone on the shores of Tanganyika had roused his interest in the deep secrets of the Dark Continent, and when the life-work of the old explorer was over, he started off with enthusiasm to carry it on.

"I have opened the door," Livingstone had said; "I leave it to you to see that no one closes it after me."

"I am ready to be, if God wills it, the next martyr to geographical science," Stanley affirmed.

Arrived at Zanzibar, he marched to the southern shore of Victoria Nyanza. Here he put together the sections of an English boat, which he launched on the lake, and in the "Lady Alice," he made his famous circumnavigation. He proved once for all, that the Nile left it at its northern end, and for 300 miles raced between high rocky walls over rapids and cataracts, till it passed into the Albert Nyanza and out of it northwards to Khartum. The river and two lakes formed the boundary of Uganda, the "Pearl of Africa," which country Stanley now entered. He was warmly received by the king, Mtesa.

"My mother dreamt a dream," said Mtesa with confidence, "and she saw a white man on this lake in a boat coming this way, and lo, you have come!"

The country ruled over by this king was large and fertile, but the people were uncivilised, and executions for slight offences took place daily, by the orders of the king. Stanley was greatly struck by the intelligence of the king—he at once grasped the possibilities of Uganda as a centre of civilisation for the surrounding country.

"I see in Mtesa the light that shall lighten the darkness of this benighted region," he wrote home. "With his aid the civilisation of equatorial Africa becomes possible."

He translated parts of the Bible into a language that the king could read, and so earnestly did he relate the story of Christ, that the king ordered the Christian Sabbath to be observed throughout his realm.

"Thou shalt love thy neighbour as thyself." These words he wrote on a board in Arabic, and hung it in the palace, that all his court might read it daily. The explorer now wrote home a glowing account of Uganda, and begged that missionaries might be sent without delay. They must belong to no particular nation, no sect or Church; but in the midst of these pagan peoples, they must lead the blameless lives of Christians. The appeal arrived at a time when Europe was keenly interested in Africa, and at once a party of Protestants made their way to Uganda, together with a party of Roman Catholics from France.

In 1884 Mtesa died, and was succeeded by his son Mwanga. He hated all Europeans, and resolved to rid the country of them. The English bishop, Hannington, was murdered, together with forty of his followers, while the native converts were burned. It seemed as if this fair country must relapse, when an Englishman, now Sir Frederick Lugard, saved the situation. He had just returned from the Burmese wars, when he volunteered for service under the British East Africa Company, which was establishing a protectorate over the country south of the Egyptian Sudan, and east of the great lakes towards the coast. It seems strange to hear of an Englishman freeing slaves at Mombasa and Melinda, ports of Vasco da Gama fame; but the slave trade at this time was cruelly carried on by natives in these parts. Lugard's work on the coast was suddenly interrupted by orders to go in hot haste to Uganda, over which country a British protectorate was being formed. Lugard reached the capital a few days before Christmas 1890. Matters were in a critical state. Arms and ammunition were on the way to the king, Mwanga, whose intention was to murder all Europeans. Meanwhile English and French, or Protestants and Roman Catholics, strove for the mastery. Lugard saw the king. He made it clear that the whole country was now British, and that, under the British flag, all religion was free, and a treaty to this effect must be signed at once by the king. On Christmas eve he presented the treaty at the king's court. Mwanga was trembling with terror. Lugard was persuading him to sign, when suddenly a clamour arose from a crowd at the door, and angry voices murmured that every man who signed the treaty would be shot. There was the clicking of rifles and the cocking of guns.

It was a critical moment in the history of Uganda. Another moment would have seen bloodshed. Lugard pressed the matter no further that day. Amid shouts and angry voices from the French Roman Catholics, he quietly withdrew. Next day was Christmas. Lugard, after an anxious night, again sought an interview with the king. But as he neared the royal residence, drums rattled, and armed men with rifles stole about the grounds. Once more he turned back, amid the jeers of the rabble. But Lugard was a resolute man, and next morning he succeeded in getting the treaty signed without bloodshed.

It was some time before the country was sufficiently restored to peace, but on April 1, 1893, the British flag was hoisted by Sir Gerald Portal, and from this time matters have progressed rapidly, and a new era of peace and progress dawned on Uganda.

In 1902 a railway was completed from Mombasa to Victoria Nyanza, which to-day is being carried farther and farther into the heart of Eastern Africa. So the dream of General Gordon has been fulfilled, and the Sudan is connected by rail and telegraph with Uganda and the coast, while men are still scheming to accomplish the grander dream of Cecil Rhodes—the connection of the Cape and Cairo by rail and telegraph—

"Ay, one land
From Lion's Head to Line."

CHAPTER 36

THE FOUNDING OF RHODESIA

"We were dreamers, dreaming greatly,
in the man-stifled town;
We yearned beyond the sky-line,
where the strange roads go down."
—KIPLING.

LET us see how this Cape to Cairo scheme sprung into being by the founding of Rhodesia by Rhodes.

The Transvaal State emerged from its war of independence penniless, but the old arrangements were soon set to work again, and the new President formed plans for enlarging his boundaries. Bands of Boer raiders entered the neighbouring territory of Bechuanaland to the west, and established themselves around Vryburg to the north of Kimberley and Griqualand West. This country was the open door to Central Africa discovered by Livingstone. If the Transvaal established a protectorate over Bechuanaland, what would become of Cecil Rhodes' dream of a great northern empire, stretching to the Zambesi and beyond? He now raised his voice and cried to his country to act at once.

216

"Soon, soon it may be too late!" he cried in tones that demanded attention.

England listened, and in 1885 proclaimed her protectorate over Bechuanaland. The road to the interior was now open.

Stretching away northwards, beyond the Limpopo or Crocodile river, which forms the northern boundary of the Transvaal, is a vast country, which now forms part of the British Empire, under the name of its founder, Rhodesia. It was little known at this time. A few explorers and hunters had brought back glowing accounts of healthy uplands, well-watered valleys, and abundance of gold. The country south of the Zambesi was inhabited by native tribes, known as the Mashonas and Matabilis, under the rule of King Lobengula.

One day in the year 1888, three adventurous young Englishmen visited him at his royal kraal at Buluwayo. They came to obtain his leave for the sole right to search for the minerals within his territory. With some difficulty they obtained it, and carried the joyful news back to Cape Colony. Preparations went forward, and a band of pioneers was soon ready to advance into the new country of Mashonaland.

In olden days the march of the Ten Thousand thrilled the ancients with admiration. In modern times no more heroic march has been performed than this by the Mashonaland Pioneers, who cut their way through a thousand miles of roadless country inhabited by a warlike and powerful race of savage tribes. Dressed in brown corduroy tunics and trousers, with leather leggings and "Buffalo Bill" hats, they started off in the summer of 1890. By May they had reached and crossed the Limpopo, and were in the country of the Matabilis. Every precaution was taken in case of attack from these savage warriors. The long train of waggons, each drawn by sixteen oxen, was led by mounted troopers. At night a laager was made of waggons, with a maxim gun at each corner, while an electric search-light lit up the dark sky and kept the terrified Matabili at a safe distance. Marching steadily forwards, the Pioneers reached the Tull river on July 1. They had now to cut their way through thick forest, till a month later, they arrived at the top of the tableland and beheld a sight which gladdened their hearts. Before them spread open grassy downs, where the town of Victoria stands to-day. Five months after leaving Cape Town, the Pioneers were in the very heart of Mashonaland, and the British flag was flying over a spot called Fort Salisbury, in honour of the Imperial Prime Minister. A rush for the gold-fields soon took place, and "Golden Mashonaland" became a second El Dorado. Old gold mines were discovered with remains of Phoenician civilisation, and the question arose: "Was not this the Ophir of Solomon's days?"

Under the Chartered Company, which resembled the old East India Company, colonisation went on apace, under the administration of Rhodes' old friend, Dr Jameson. Till one day in July 1893, the news spread that the Matabili army had entered Mashonaland, and the white men were no longer safe. An expedition was prepared by Dr Jameson, backed by Cecil Rhodes; and some thousand colonists in three columns marched forth against one of the most powerful tribes in South Africa. As the force advanced towards Lobengula's capital at Buluwayo, the Matabilis retreated across the Shangani river, which divided Mashonaland from Matabililand. The colonial troops were advancing, when early one morning a loud report rent the air. It was followed by huge columns of smoke rising from Buluwayo, where a store of gun-powder had been blown up by the panic-stricken inhabitants, who with Lobengula were now flying from before the face of the white men.

A party of 300 men, under Major Forbes, was at once sent in pursuit of the king. The success of the capture depended on speed. So on December 3, Major Allan Wilson, with a small party of well-mounted men, were sent on rapidly across the Shangani river in pursuit of Lobengula. He was to return before night to the camp. But when evening fell, Wilson found that the king was but six miles ahead of him, so he sent a messenger back to Forbes to beg for reinforcements without delay, as the Matabili were very strong.

The night was dark, and rain was falling fast. There was no sleep for the men of Wilson's patrol in the midst of foes, no sleep either for Forbes with preparations for an early start forwards. But at daybreak it was discovered that the Shangani had risen in the night and it was impossible to cross. Further, a large force of Matabili now attacked the men in camp, and all hopes of joining Wilson had to be given up. The little patrol party must be left to their fate. That fate was learnt later from the Matabili warriors. At dawn, Wilson had made a dash for the king's person, but a tremendous fire had suddenly opened upon the little party, from a band of Matabili hidden in the bush. The handful of Englishmen fell back on a large mound. Here they dismounted and formed a ring with their horses, behind which they took shelter. There was no request for quarter, no thought of surrender. With "iron calmness" the men fought on for two long hours, till their ammunition gave out. As soon as the supreme moment came, those who were yet able to rise, stood shoulder to shoulder and lifted their hats. Then, said the Matabili afterwards—then they joined in a song—the missionaries sang to the natives—probably "God save the Queen," and singing, died. Still one man was left, upright, hopeful, brave to the last. Alone he stood in the midst of the dead bodies of his comrades, a hero among heroes, and single-handed he fought the foe, till he too fell dead at the last. The desperate bravery of Wilson's heroic band struck the natives with awe and reverence. To-day the spot is marked by a wonderful bas-relief, sent by Cecil Rhodes, but no memorial is needed to keep the story fresh in the minds of his countrymen. "For it is by such men that the Empire has been made."

"Because on the bones of the English,
the English flag is stayed."

Soon after this Lobengula died, the Matabili submitted, and the British flag waved over Buluwayo. The new country was won and named after the man, who had not only dreamed of a northern empire, but made it possible for his country to conquer and colonise it.

CHAPTER 37

BRITISH SOUTH AFRICA

"Together, sundered once by blood and speech,
 Joined here in equal muster of the brave,
 Lie Boer and Briton, foes each worthy each.
 May peace strike root into their common grave,
 And blossoming where the fathers fought and died,
 Bear fruit for sons that labour side by side."
 —EDMUND GARRETT (in the Monthly Review).

WHILE progress and the fruits of civilisation followed the Mashonaland Pioneers to golden Rhodesia, the Transvaal under its President, Paul Kruger, still pursued its old-fashioned mode of life. Severed from Europe two hundred years before, the Boers clung tenaciously to the ideas of their ancestors. Their religion was that of the seventeenth century, rigid and stern. They had few books and newspapers: they were ignorant of much that was passing in the world beyond. Two hundred years of solitary pastoral life had given them a distaste for commerce and industry, so that when, in 1884, a sudden swarm of gold-diggers flocked into their country, they went on their way unaffected by the movement.

Meanwhile the new-comers, by hundreds and thousands, made their way to the high veld south of Pretoria—to the Witwatersrand, or the white water ridge, where they found gold in abundance. Soon Johannesburg—the "city of the golden reef"—sprang up in the midst of the famous gold-fields, and the treasury of the Transvaal grew full to overflowing. From this time onwards, Europeans flocked to the golden city, until they became more numerous than the Boers themselves. In their own countries—England, Germany, France—these Europeans, or Outlanders, as they were called by the Dutch, had been accustomed to have a voice in public affairs; and this they now demanded of Paul Kruger. But the President disliked the intrusion of foreigners in his country. He thought that to give them a voice in the government meant ruin to the ancient customs of his forefathers. He feared the tide of modern ideas, which was even now lapping nearer and ever nearer, and which must, in due course, flow over his land too at the last.

As time went on, the voices of the Outlanders grew louder: their grievances increased. "Reform! reform!" they cried persistently. But the old President was firm. He would concede nothing to these Outlanders—nothing. He could not be brought to see that the very principle of acting in accordance with the wishes of the people, which had induced England to forego her dominion over the Transvaal, now pointed to new conditions of government, in which Outlanders and Dutch should have equal political rights.

223

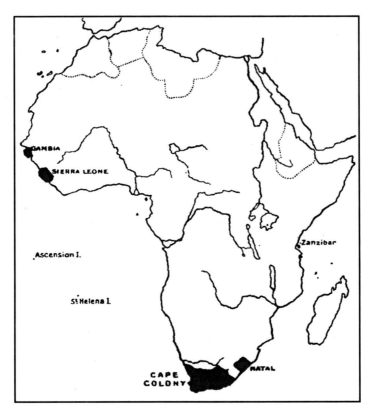

British possessions in Africa, 1837.

British possessions in Africa, 1903.

"Africa," said Herodotus of old, "is a land of surprises."

A surprise was now in store for all. It was the end of December 1895. Some of the Outlanders, tired of their vain efforts to obtain justice by other means, planned rebellion. They were in communication with Cecil Rhodes, Prime Minister at the Cape, and Dr Jameson, Administrator of Rhodesia. Dr Jameson had collected a small force at Mafeking, on the Transvaal borders, and agreed with the Outlanders to join them on a given day, to take possession of Johannesburg and seize the arsenal at Pretoria. He sadly underrated the intelligence, the courage, the infinite resource of the Boers, and started off with his troops, only to be met at Krugersdorp by a strong force of Boers under General Cronje, to whom he had to surrender. The raid deservedly failed. Punishment in England was meted out to Dr Jameson and his officers, the Johannesburg Outlanders were heavily fined by the Transvaal Government, and Cecil Rhodes resigned his position as Prime Minister of the Cape and retired to Rhodesia.

But no punishment could undo the evil that had been done. Kruger was sterner than ever with the Outlanders, and a Government, elected by only one class of the population, was carried on. Arms for the Dutch burghers now poured into the Transvaal in ever-increasing quantities. Rapidly and feverishly, preparations for inevitable war were pushed on, until 1899. It was a question of who was to be supreme in South Africa.

"Africa for the Africanders!" cried the Dutch.

"Equal rights for all white men!" cried the English.

It was an impossible state of affairs. A conference between Lord Milner and Mr Kruger—representatives of England and the Transvaal—led to no result. In the autumn of 1899, war was declared by the Boers. The storm-cloud that had hung over the country for so long had burst at last. The story of the South African war need not be told again. The resistance was splendid, but the end was certain. The tide of modern thought that the President had stayed through the long years of his Presidency, swept over the Transvaal and Orange Free State at the last, and Paul Kruger fled to Europe.

But the great statesman, who had seen from the first that progress and modern ideas of government were bound up with a British South Africa, lay sleeping his last sleep amid the Matoppo hills in Rhodesia. Before peace was proclaimed, Cecil Rhodes had died in the land of his adoption. With all his faults, he was the greatest statesman South Africa has ever seen; with all his limitations, he was cast in "heroic mould, with an impulse towards noble ends." A "dreamer devout by vision led, beyond our guess or reach," his ideas were colossal, his outlook on life was vast, his strength magnificent. One purpose ran through his life, and he worked with all his manhood's power to achieve that purpose.

His wish to be buried among the Matoppo hills above Buluwayo, looking forth "across the lands he won," was characteristic of the man's solitary grandeur; and as the long procession wound amid the hills and valleys of Rhodesia, even the natives dimly realised that a great man had passed from their midst.

"The immense and brooding spirit still
Shall quicken and control;
Living, he was the land; and dead,
His soul shall be her soul."

Within two months of his death, in 1902, peace was declared.

To-day Boer and Briton stand shoulder to shoulder, "forged in strong fires, by equal war made one," both members of one great Empire; and as time rolls onward into space, they may feel

"The touch of human brotherhood, and act
As one great nation, true and strong as steel."

CHAPTER 38

THE DOMINION OF CANADA

"So long as the Blood endures,
I shall know that your good is mine;
ye shall feel that my strength is yours."
—KIPLING.

A QUARTER of a century had passed away, since the union of the two Canadas by Lord Durham. In the joint Parliament, Upper and Lower Canada were equally represented. This was all very well for a time, but Upper Canada had been increasing rapidly, until now it not only exceeded a million inhabitants, but it exceeded the population of Lower Canada.

"Let us have representation according to the number of our population," cried the British settlers in Upper Canada.

Canada had thus reached a critical stage in her history, when she learned that the three Atlantic colonies—Nova Scotia, New Brunswick, and Prince Edward Island—were already considering the idea of a union among themselves. Canada asked leave to join them. Representatives from the four colonies sat in Quebec. For eighteen days they discussed the welfare of the colonies with closed doors. A good understanding was arrived at, and a scheme for a great federal union of all British North America "leapt suddenly from the realm of dreams into the forefront of practical politics."

On the historic ground of old Quebec, where but a century before, English and French had fought out their great battle for supremacy, the sons of both now agreed on a final scheme of union. Their resolution was followed by the Queen's declaration that "on and after July 1, 1867, the provinces of Canada, Nova Scotia, and New Brunswick shall be one dominion under the name of Canada."

So at the stroke of midnight on June 30, the old order passed away, and dawn ushered in the new Dominion of Canada. Upper Canada henceforth was to be known as the province of Ontario, Lower Canada as the province of Quebec.

Amid the booming of cannon and the beating of drums, the whole country burst into song—

"Canada, Canada! land of the bravest!
Sons of the war-path and sons of the sea!
Bells chime out merrily,
Trumpets call cheerily,
Let the sky ring with the shout of the free!"

Meanwhile the transfer of land to the Dominion brought trouble in its train, and the Red River rebellion threatened to destroy the peace of Canada for a time. Under Louis Riel, the colonists rose to protect their lands, which they ignorantly supposed would be taken from them. The Red River Settlement, founded by Lord Selkirk, was in the very heart of the Dominion, equidistant from Pacific and Atlantic coasts. It was difficult enough to march an army thither from Quebec, but Colonel Wolseley, in command of 1200 picked men, made his way through 600 miles of water and forest, reaching the rebellious settlement to find Louis Riel had fled. Order was soon established, and Manitoba joined the union peacefully.

With the addition of Manitoba, British Columbia, and the North-West Territories, the Dominion of Canada stretched 3000 miles from sea to sea. The little British possession of 1759, described by the French as "a few square miles of snow," had grown, till she was thirty times the size of the mother country. Newfoundland—the oldest colony of all—alone stands aloof, bearing her burdens alone. Some day she may think fit to join the federal union, and the dream of colonial statesmen will be realised.

The Government of Canada to-day is federal—that is, there is a central Government sitting at Ottawa and arranging the affairs of the whole Dominion, while a local Parliament presides over each provincial capital. And the whole is under the British flag and the British king to-day.

When federation took place, the only British route to Quebec and Ontario was by way of the St Lawrence river, closed by ice for half the year. A

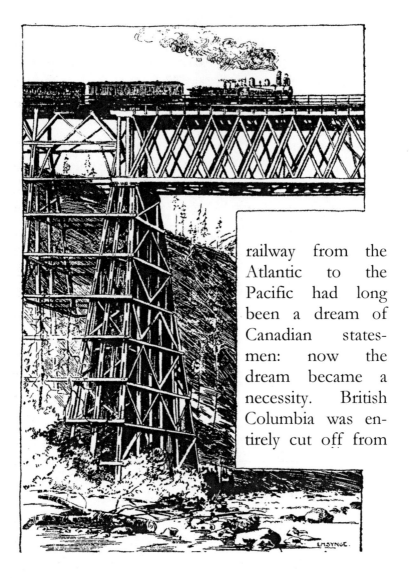

railway from the Atlantic to the Pacific had long been a dream of Canadian statesmen: now the dream became a necessity. British Columbia was entirely cut off from

her sister provinces in the east, and until the vast west lands were brought into closer communication with one another, federation could only be a name. The young nation rose finely to its responsibilities, as it promoted a scheme for the now famous Canadian-Pacific railway, before which the richest empire in

Europe might have quailed. Much of the country through which the line would pass, was unexplored. Deep lakes and mighty rivers, vast plains and high mountain-ranges, opposed the progress of the engineers. But perseverance won the day. The Canadian-Pacific railway, 3000 miles in length, was triumphantly opened on Dominion Day 1886, and still remains one of the greatest engineering feats the world has ever seen. Leaving Quebec and Montreal, the train passes the political capital of Ottawa. From Ottawa to Winnipeg, on the Red river, it makes its way through some 1300 miles of forest and lake country. Leaving wheat-growing Manitoba, it runs through some 800 miles of prairie,—treeless, monotonous, lonely,—till at Calgary, the ascent of the Rocky Mountains begins. Through the gorges and over the passes of the snow-capped Rockies, the train now winds its careful way—up and ever upwards, amid awful precipices and steep forest-clad mountains. The deep blue sky, the green flash of the glaciers, the white gleam of the snow and the rush of foaming waters, add splendour to the scene, till, at last, the Great Divide is reached on the summit. Then, by way of the Kicking Horse Pass, the descent begins; and through a region of gigantic firs and cedars, Vancouver, the great western terminus, is reached. Here are the great steamers that cross the Pacific to Japan in ten days.

And to-day emigrants are flocking to Canada, the Granary of England, to develop more and more the wheat-growing districts, which cry aloud for the honest toil of her sons and daughters, to yield of the richest and best.

"Shall not we, through good and ill,
   Cleave to one another still?
   Britain's myriad voices call:
   'Sons be welded, each and all,
   Into one Imperial whole;
   One with Britain, heart and soul—
   One life, one flag, one fleet, one throne.' "

CHAPTER 39

AUSTRALIA—THE NEW NATION

"The Law that ye make shall be law,
and I do not press my will,
Because ye are Sons of the Blood,
and call me Mother still."
—KIPLING.

NOT only did the Canadian-Pacific railway draw together the various provinces in the Dominion of Canada, but it drew the distant island continent of Australia closer to the mother country.

Let us see how Australia had prospered, since the days of her early colonisation, and how gradually she adopted the same form of government as her sister colony Canada.

Eight years had passed away, since Eyre had heroically forced his way across the 1500 miles of waste, stretching across the southern colonies. Australia was suffering from poverty and want of more hardy emigrants, when the gold rush took place to California. Among others, an Australian colonist, Hargreaves, was smitten with the gold-fever, and made his way to America, to be struck with the great similarity of the two countries.

"Slate, quartz, granite," he argued to himself; "if these mean gold country in America, why not in New South Wales?"

Returning home in 1851, he made his way across the Blue Mountains from Sydney to Bathurst, and was rewarded by finding gold in a creek, which he named Ophir, after the famous old diggings of King Solomon. A rush of diggers took place, until the mountain road from Sydney to Bathurst was thronged with men from all parts of Australia. The neighbouring colony of Victoria was in danger of losing all its colonists, as they flocked off in search of gold, when suddenly the news spread of still richer gold-fields within twenty miles of Melbourne. A yet wilder rush took place. Melbourne became a deserted city. Shops were shut, the plough rusted in the furrow, shearing-time came and there were no shearers. The Governor at Melbourne ruled "in pathetic loneliness—a monarch without a realm."

As the news spread, emigrants from England and America flocked into the country. In two years a quarter of a million people arrived in Victoria for this "Working Man's Paradise." The colonies grew apace. Railways sprang into being, telegraph poles stretched from town to town, and the government of the five separate colonies was re-adjusted to suit the new demands.

A new impetus was given to exploration: men realised how little was yet known of the interior of their great continent, and with the increase of population had come the desire for expansion. So the rich little colony of Victoria fitted out an expedition to attempt an overland route from south to north, from sea to sea. This expedition of Burke and Wills across Australia is one of the most famous in the annals of Australian exploration. The men of Melbourne turned out in their thousands to see the little band of men under their chosen leader, Burke, start on their great journey. The whole expedition had been carefully prepared. Camels had been brought from India to make the desert journey easier; a waggon had been constructed which, with its wheels off, would make a punt for crossing rivers. No pains had been spared. The party reached Cooper's Creek, near the boundary of New South Wales and Queensland, in safety on November 11. It was an old and well-known camping-ground in the midst of a flat sandy plain, through which a river wound its way. After a month spent here, Burke divided his party of eight into two, determined to push on for the northern coast.

"Wait here till we come back," he said to the four remaining at Cooper's Creek. "We may be three months; we may be four."

"We will wait," was the firm reply.

So, on December 16, Burke and Wills, King and Gray, with six camels, one horse, and food for three months, started off for the unknown. After two months of toilsome travel, they reached the salt water of the Gulf of Carpentaria. Within fifty miles of the coast they turned back, for provisions were running short and the way was arduous and long. They had been the first men to cross Australia from sea to sea, but the journey back was rich in disaster. Rains had made the ground heavy; the camels, tired with overwork and little food, sank down and died. Food ran so short that the hungry explorers had to kill and eat their poor tired horse, Billy. At last, on the 21st of April, Burke, Wills, and King (for Gray was dead) dragged themselves wearily back to Cooper's Creek. All was silent and deserted; and as the awful truth dawned on them, Burke threw himself on to the ground in despair, while Wills sobbed out: "They are gone."

On a tree was cut the word "Dig." Obeying, they found a bottle, inside which was a paper with these words: "We leave the camp to-day, April 21, 1861. We have left you some food, but take camels and horses."

That very day, perhaps but a few hours since, the party, after waiting four months and five days, had left for home. The weary explorers were too tired to follow, too sick at heart to think. They ate some oatmeal and sugar, and two days later, struggled on their way once more. At last their food failed. They ate a black seed called nardoo, cooked by the natives, but they grew weaker and weaker. Wills succumbed first. Heroically he insisted that his two friends should push on, as their only chance of safety, while he lay down to die alone. A few days later Burke died too, and King alone lived to stagger

Death of Burke

back to Melbourne with the news of their success, which was dearly bought.

To-day telegraph posts stretch from sea to sea, and men are developing the inheritance won through so much courage and endurance by their fellow-countrymen.

Still the passing years found the five great colonies and Tasmania distinct and separate, each clinging blindly to its own individual existence. Australia was a continent of quarrelling colonies, with petty jealousies, bitter feelings, and a short-sighted outlook on the vast possibilities of the future. It was not till the end of the nineteenth century, that in the face of a common danger, the desirability of uniting their country took hold of men's minds.

"How could we defend our coasts in the event of an attack?" the colonists asked themselves hopelessly. The idea of federation grew. In 1891 a great convention was held at Sydney to discuss this idea.

"The crimson thread of kinship runs through us all," cried Sir Harry Parkes at a banquet of representatives from the various colonies and New Zealand. The difficulties seemed unsurmountable. Nine long years passed by, and it was not till 1900, that it was finally decided to break down all barriers and to merge the separate life of the five states and Tasmania into one joint dominion under the broad flag of Great Britain.

The news thrilled through every fibre of the world-wide Empire. The queen of the mother country sent out her grandson, now the heir-apparent to the British throne, to open the first Federal Parliament for her sons beyond the sea. It was a memorable day in the history of Australia, when the great white Ophir steamed into Melbourne harbour bearing the British Prince and Princess to distant Australian shores. The opening of Parliament took place on May 9, 1901, amid the greatest enthusiasm, and messages soon flashed to every quarter of the globe with the news, that Australia had entered on a new era of existence.

Australia—the Great South Land of past years—has at last awakened to her great duties and responsibilities. For the first time in history one nation occupies a whole continent; and that island continent, now ranking as one of the world-powers, is putting forth her splendid energies to work out mighty destinies, under the flag of the mother country.

CHAPTER 40

FREEDOM FOR CUBA

"With Freedom's soil beneath our feet
And Freedom's banner floating o'er us."
—DRAKE.

THE story of this conflict between Spain and America is one of the most pathetic in the world's modern history, for it shows how utterly fallen from her high estate was the once glorious Spanish nation.

The discovery of America by Columbus had given Spain a territory, which might well have made her the richest empire in the world. Her soldiers were the bravest, her fleets the largest, her treasury the richest; but her lack of human sympathy had wrought her destruction. The Spanish Inquisition destroyed the very manhood of her people, and stopped the wheels of progress.

How Holland rose and drove her Spanish oppressors from the Netherlands, how England defeated the Invincible Armada, and how gradually Spain lost her vast American Empire,—these stories have been already told.

Now she was to lose her last colonies in the East and West Indies. Of these, Cuba, off the southern shores of the United States, was one. The islanders had suffered acutely from the mismanagement and cruelty of her Spanish governors. Again and again the unhappy Cubans rose against their tyrants: they were only treated more rigorously than before.

While the island was but divided from America by 100 miles of water, 3000 miles divided it from the mother country. Once the United States had proposed buying the island from Spain.

"The sale of Cuba will be the sale of Spanish honour itself," was the firm reply.

So the years rolled on, and the States, faithful to their policy of non-intervention, looked on sadly and patiently. But the state of Cuba grew from bad to worse. Its horrors were worthy the days of Cortes and Pizarro. Thousands died within Spanish prison walls in a few months; little children died in the streets from starvation; homes were in ruins; the beautiful island was laid desolate.

On the evening of February 15, 1898, matters reached a crisis. For some weeks past, the American ship, the Maine, had been lying in the harbour of Havana at the north end of the island. Suddenly, as evening wore to night, a terrific explosion occurred, and the Maine sank, carrying down with her 266 of her crew. A great wave of anger swept over the States, and soon the whole nation was clamouring for war. It was no war of aggression, no war of revenge. Never did a people willingly shed their blood in a more disinterested cause or with more lofty aims. It was a war for humanity—to make an oppressed people free and independent.

Within a fortnight of the declaration of war between the United States and Spain, the first blow was struck in the far East Indies, where an attack was made on the Philippine Islands by Admiral Dewey, of the United States navy. Six ships of the American fleet were cruising in the Pacific Ocean, when war was declared. The Spanish fleet lay at Manila, the capital of the Spanish possessions in the East. How Admiral Dewey courageously led his ships at dead of night, in single file, through the unknown and perilous passage leading to the harbour of Manila, is now a well-known story. The harbour was protected by submarine mines; the shore bristled with Spanish batteries; the Spanish fleet outnumbered that of the United States; and, behind all, was a city of 300,000 people. It was an adventure which savoured of the olden times. On through the darkness crept the American ships. Just before the break of dawn, the moon broke through the clouds. The advancing ships were close to Manila. It was Sunday morning, May 1, when the Spanish ships, flying their battle-flags of red and gold, opened fire on the Americans.

"When you are ready, you may fire," said Admiral Dewey to his Captain, as the flag-ship Olympia came within range of the Spanish guns.

Soon the air was full of smoke and shells as, amid the roar of guns, the new nation and the old fought for freedom. The Spaniards were brave to the death, but American skill and science was too much for them. By midday, the destruction of the Spanish fleet was complete. Admiral Dewey had lost neither ship nor man. It was the most wonderful triumph of the American fleet in American history. It showed Europe, that the United States as a naval power was formidable; it showed England, that the Viking spirit was yet alive in her sons across the seas.

So the Philippine Islands passed from the hands of Spain to the United States, under whose free government they flourish to-day.

Meanwhile another Spanish fleet, under Admiral Cervera, had secretly made its way to Cuba. It was lying quietly in the harbour of Santiago, protected by frowning batteries, while a network of submarine torpedoes lined the bottle-shaped harbour, and a narrow neck hid its presence.

And now followed an exploit which awoke the admiration of the whole world, and showed forth the daring heroism of America's sailors, when Lieutenant Hobson, a young naval officer, with a volunteer crew, sank the coaling-ship Merrimac, in the harbour mouth of Santiago, to bottle up the Spanish fleet. Just before dawn on the morning of June 2, 1898, Hobson and his crew, in the old collier, approached the mouth of the harbour. Instantly sheets of fire were poured on to them, by the Spanish batteries on the shore. It seemed impossible for man or ship to live through such deadly fire, but not a man was shot. Having steered the Merrimac to the appointed spot, Hobson endeavoured to swing her across the narrow channel and sink her. But already her rudder had been shot away, and she drifted rudderless with the tide, far past the narrow neck. She was sinking fast now, and as she plunged beneath the waves, her crew clung to a raft, prepared for the purpose. Only their faces were out of water. The minutes passed slowly on, till with daylight, a Spanish launch approached and took the men prisoners.

"Daring like this makes the bitterest enemy proud that his fellow-men can be such heroes," said the Spanish Admiral, shaking hands with Hobson and each of his men.

Many a brave deed was done by land and sea, before Santiago fell into the hands of the United States, and it was July 17, before the flag of the Stars and Stripes flew over Cuba, which island is independent to-day.

The war had lasted three months. It left Spain with a "few ruined hulks of what had once been a navy." It took from her the last of the colonies for which she had "sinned and suffered and struggled."

The new nation came out triumphant. Important results followed.

Enthusiasm for the United States was aroused across the seas in England. America had risen to the full sense of her manhood: she had stretched out her arms to the oppressed at her doors. And the old mother country rejoiced in her victories, and triumphed in the part she had been led to play in the world's affairs—in the cause of freedom and justice.

CHAPTER 41

REIGN OF QUEEN VICTORIA

"So hast thou won thy people's hearts; they see
Wife, mother, friend, not Queen alone, in thee."
—TENNYSON.

EVER memorable in the annals of the British Empire
is the year 1901, for, as the last rays of the sun set
over the waters of the wintry sea, that surrounded
her island home, Queen Victoria passed to her well-
won rest. It was sixty-three years since that early
June morning in 1837, when she had romantically
learnt, from the lips of her ministers, the news that
she was Queen of England. Let us see how she rose
to her responsibilities, how splendidly she struggled
with her pressing duties, until the last week of her
long reign; how pure and true her life, lived "in that
fierce light which beats upon a throne." She has left
a shining example as wife, mother, friend, for future
generations, that time shall not efface.

In the winter of 1840, she married her cousin,
Albert of Saxe-Coburg and Gotha, a young German
prince, with whom she was exceptionally happy, till
his early death, twenty-one years later, took from her

all that life held most dear. The history of her reign sums up the history of this volume. It opened with troubles in Canada and the awful disaster in the Kyber Pass in Afghanistan, both of which affected her deeply. In 1843 the Queen and the Prince Consort, leaving their three small children in England, visited France. It was the first time that an English sovereign had set foot on French soil for over 300 years, and there was much enthusiasm. Five years later, Louis Philippe and his queen were to take refuge in England on the outbreak of the Revolution of 1848. To-day, the President of the French Republic has declared his country to be the "friend of England."

Six years later, the peace of Europe was broken for the first time in the reign of Queen Victoria by the Crimean war, in which the France of Napoleon III. became England's ally against Russia. The Queen, in person, watched the departure of her soldiers for the scene of action; with her own hands she worked for their comfort during the cruel Crimean winter. Herself she welcomed home the survivors with words of gratitude, and instituted the Victoria Cross, for acts of conspicuous valour in the field.

The Indian mutiny was slowly dying out, when the marriage of her eldest daughter to the Crown Prince of Prussia took place. Her first grandson was born in 1859, and is to-day Emperor of Germany.

Slowly now the Queen was passing to the crowning sorrow of her life. The Prince Consort died in 1861. He had been her right hand, her husband, friend, critic, adviser, loved by her with a romantic and passionate devotion,—

"Two heads in council, two beside the hearth,
Two in the tangled business of the world."

Now, in a moment, the "romance of the Queen's life was changed into a tragedy." Years of desolation followed, and it was some time before the widowed Queen could steel herself, to take up alone the business of the State—the burden of Empire.

The marriage of her eldest son, the present King Edward VII., with Denmark's beautiful daughter, in 1863, was followed by the birth of Prince Albert Victor, whose tragic death on the eve of his wedding in 1892, left his sailor-brother, George, heir to the English throne.

The outbreak of civil war in America, with its tragic assassination of President Lincoln; the Mexican tragedy, in which her cousin Charlotte played so fatal a part, affected her nearly; but more near still came the Franco-German war, in which her son-in-law, the Crown Prince of Prussia, took so active a part. At the very outbreak of war, the Empress Eugenie, Napoleon's wife, who has outlived her royal friend, took refuge with Queen Victoria; but though kind to her neighbours in trouble, the Queen's sympathies were with Prussia, where her two daughters were working indefatigably to alleviate the sufferings of sick and wounded.

The Afghan campaign of 1880 was watched by the Queen with the keenest interest, while she deeply regretted the defeat of Majuba in the following year. A few months later, the death of Lord Beaconsfield, her "dear great friend" and statesman, touched her deeply. The Egyptian war followed in 1882, when her son, the Duke of Connaught, led the Guards at Tel-el-Kebir. When the policy of abandoning the Sudan was adopted by the Government under Mr Gladstone, the Queen herself urged prompt action in rescuing the isolated garrisons. She watched Gordon's advance to Khartum with the gravest concern, and the news of his "cruel but heroic fate" in 1885, caused her to feel keenly the "stain" left upon her beloved country. She kept her Jubilee of fifty years in 1887, gathering around her many sons, grandsons, daughters and grand-daughters, sons-in-law and daughters-in-law, as well as foreign representatives. One of the most conspicuous figures, towering above the rest, in white uniform, was the Crown Prince of Prussia, who the following year became Emperor of united Germany, dying of cancer three months later.

The Diamond Jubilee was kept with tremendous enthusiasm ten years later. Sorrows and joys crowded one another quickly in the Queen's life; but perhaps the war in South Africa, which broke a long and happy peace, struck the blow from which she never recovered. From that October day in 1899, when war broke out in South Africa, to the day of her death, the serious conflict occupied the chief place in her thoughts. She yearned for peace, but even this was denied her.

At the age of eighty-one, after a reign of sixty-three years, Queen Victoria passed away. No sovereign was ever more deeply mourned. From every corner of the vast Empire, that had grown during her reign, came expressions of the deepest sorrow. Her long life, her great troubles, her sympathy in the welfare of her subjects, her unflinching devotion to the arduous duties of the State,—these had won their way into the hearts of the people. From end to end of the world went up a cry of sorrow, for nearly every nation had lost a friend in the Queen of the British Empire, though none could grudge her that bravely-earned rest— "the goal of this great world" which "lies beyond our sight."

CHAPTER 42

WELDING THE EMPIRE

"Sons be welded, each and all,
   Into one Imperial whole;
   One with Britain, heart and soul—
   One life, one flag, one fleet, one throne."
                              —TENNYSON.

IN the beginning of the nineteenth century, communication was slow and difficult, not only between town and town, but also between country and country. The introduction of penny post, railway, and telegraph ushered in a new era into the world's history—a new era, too, in the history of England, whose Empire plays so large a part in the progress of the world to-day.

Into the position she now holds, she has sprung within the memory of man, by reason of her success in colonisation.

If communication between town and town was difficult, between the mother country and the colonies it was laborious indeed. In early Victorian days, the colonies were regarded as "inconvenient encumbrances"; indeed, one Colonial Secretary had so little idea of the geography of the colonies he had undertaken to govern, that he begged a friend to get some maps and show him "where the places were." When a British emigrant left his native shores he sailed in the old wooden three-decker, never to return. It was the ready substitution of steamers for sailing-ships, that gave England a rapid lead over other nations. With her ready reserve of coal and iron, large commercial interests, her realm "bound in with the triumphant sea," she built hastily and competed successfully with Europe and America. This bridging over of the rough ocean seas, this shortening of distance from shore to shore, brought the colonies within measurable distance of the mother country, until to-day Canada can be reached by steamer in seven days, South Africa in fifteen days, India in sixteen days, and Australia in thirty-five days.

With this growing annihilation of space, England was free to carry on her great mission for which she was so well fitted—of carrying freedom, justice, and equity across the broad seas. She sent forth her sons to their distant homes, knowing they would be true-born Britons to the end. France had her colonies, Germany had hers; but for various reasons, they had not the vigorous growth permitted to those, which to-day form so large a part of the British Empire. Still England seemed utterly indifferent to her colonies at this time: even the union of Canada in 1867 stirred no enthusiasm in the mother country. Australia, India, New Zealand,

and the lesser possessions were treated as foreign countries.

It was the Queen herself, who led the way to the new idea of welding the colonies closer to the mother country: she was one of the first to realise the glorious heritage upon which she had entered, with its great message of freedom and hope,—

> "Because ye are Sons of the Blood,
> and call me Mother still."

Her proclamation as Empress of India in 1877 brought that country into closer touch with England. Dusky Indians were brought over to guard their Empress, which they did to the end with the most faithful devotion; while, among her manifold pressing duties, she laboriously tried to learn their language.

In 1884 Canadian boatmen took part in Lord Wolseley's expedition up the Nile to the relief of Gordon, while the following year New South Wales enthusiastically offered a contingent.

"Men, horses, and guns are ready to start," they wrote, "and we desire to pay the cost."

From this time onwards, the colonists have bravely taken their share in the troubles of their mother country. Yet a further step was gained, when the Indian and Colonial Exhibition was opened in London in 1886, at which an amazing display of the vast resources of the Empire revealed the unknown to wondering Britons. Great enthusiasm prevailed, and more than one poet burst into song:

> "To-day we seek to bind in one,
>   Till all our Britain's work be done;
>   Through wider knowledge closer grown,
>   As each fair sister by the rest is known."

A new spirit of brotherhood dawned, and past indifference gave way to an ever increasing interest well described by Kipling—

> "Those that have staid at thy knees,
>   Mother, go call them in;
>   We that were bred over-seas,
>   wait and would speak with our kin.
>
>   .   .   .   .
>
>   Hear, for thy children speak from
>   the uttermost parts of the sea."

As time went on the idea of union grew and grew, till in 1887, at the Queen's Jubilee, an Imperial note was struck, and the bond of Empire immensely strengthened.

In the magnificent procession through the great capital of the British Empire at the Queen's Diamond Jubilee in 1897, passed subjects from every corner of the vast inheritance on which "the sun never sets." There were richly-clad Indians, stalwart Maoris from New Zealand, lancers from Tasmania and the Australian colonies, troops from Canada, Cape Mounted Rifles, Natal volunteers. There were

yeomen from Trinidad, artillery from Malta and
Jamaica, Haussas from West Africa, Dyak police
from North Borneo, men from the Straits
Settlements, Hong-kong, and Ceylon, while the
Premiers from the self-governing colonies were
cheered to the echo by their grateful countrymen in
England. When war broke out, two years later,
between England and the Republics in South Africa,
offers of help poured in from the colonies, to be
gratefully accepted by the mother country.

> "Let this thing be. Who shall our realm divide?
> Ever we stand together, Kinsmen, side by side."

Meanwhile science too was at work welding
this great Empire. By means of submarine cables,
already messages were rapidly transmitted from
country to country. The scheme for an All-British
submarine cable had long been under discussion, but
it had been coldly looked upon till Mr. Chamberlain,
as Colonial Secretary, regarded it as part of his
Imperial policy. Then suddenly was fulfilled the
prophecy of Shakspere's Puck: "I'll put a girdle
round the earth in forty minutes." At three o'clock
on October 31, 1902, the last link in the All-British
Pacific submarine cable was completed, and
messages from Australia to England can be
transmitted in an hour instead of a day. The practical
use of electricity, as a means of communication, is
rapidly annihilating space to-day; while one of the
most wonderful inventions of the age is Marconi's
wireless telegraphy, by which ships at sea can be

communicated with, and the fleet summoned in case of danger.

Thus briefly we have sketched the change of feeling, that came over the relation of the mother country to her colonies during the nineteenth century. Distant and isolated possessions are fast developing into a united Empire, the bonds of which must of necessity be drawn closer and closer.

But an Empire "broad-based upon the people's will," resting not alone on arms or force or trade, but on the men who have created it, is perhaps the finest example of Imperialism yet known to mankind.

Let us now see how it lies with the men and women of the future—joint heirs and partners in the glories and traditions of the British Empire, to be good citizens of their vast inheritance.

CHAPTER 43

CITIZENSHIP

"Be great in act as you have been in thought;
Grow great by your example, and put on
The dauntless spirit of resolution."
—SHAKSPERE.

IT has just been stated that the British Empire depends on the men and women, who have themselves created it. Therefore it is of vast importance that the boys and girls of to-day— subjects of the king, inheritors of the Empire, makers of the future—should rightly understand their responsibilities.

The prosperity of a free nation depends, not on its king and rulers only, but mainly on its people—on every single individual who dwells under the protection of its flag. Every grown man, with certain qualifications, has a vote—that is, a voice in the government of the country. He controls taxation, directs commerce, and regulates the relationships of his country with foreign lands. But how can he do this well, if he does not know the history of his own country and her relations with the great world around her?

"What do they know of England
Who only England know?"

A man cannot exercise his full powers unless he has been educated, or learnt for himself the past history of his own country and those with which she is connected. So that "knowledge of the road by which we have come may indicate the line of further advance."

Hence one of the great duties of a citizen lies in the attainment of education. It is a vital interest, and on it the fate of the Empire may hang. "Knowledge is power." Nothing is more dangerous than ignorance. Every mother who sends her child regularly to school is strengthening the nation; every child who learns diligently is struggling to become a good citizen; every single-hearted teacher is working for the good of mankind, and the welfare of the Empire.

Germany has become a great power, by reason of her keen interest in education and her industry. The same spirit has dominated the United States of America, where the best possible teaching has been secured for all.

True education does not make a man proud: rather, as Plato remarked long years ago, "You will be soberer and humbler and gentler to other men, not fancying you know what you do not know."

It fits a man for the battle of life, for when school-days are done, there is still much left to learn: there are new methods to be adopted, new inventions to be studied, new ideas to be entertained.

"The old country must wake up," said the Prince of Wales on his return from his colonial tour in 1901, "if she intends to maintain her old position of pre-eminence in her colonial trade against foreign competition."

The old country cannot wake up, unless every individual awakes to this necessity.

Education is much, but not all. Honest work, well done, is building up the nation's power and strengthening her manhood. Here again each must play his part. As each stick is needed to make up a faggot, so the work of each member of a community is necessary to ensure success. The commanding general receives applause for a brilliant victory, but he acknowledges the essential part played by his subordinates. It has been said that the battle of Omdurman was won in the workshops of Wady Halfa. Victory abroad is due to good work done in the iron-foundries at home,—due to those who manufacture the soldiers' boots and fill their cartridges, due to the hard-working engineer of the railway line, just as much as to the courage of the soldiers who fight in the field. It is hard to overrate the importance of small things, but for every plank laid straight, every button firmly stitched, every boot well soled, the nation, is better and stronger.

"In all true work," says Carlyle, "were it but true hand-labour, there is something of divineness. Labour has its summit in heaven."

Then the good citizen will love his country. He will glory in her old traditions of freedom and justice, he will strive to maintain them for his children and his children's children. Ready to learn for her, ready to work for her, he will be ready, if need be, to fight for her.

England's navy is her "all-in-all"; but she keeps a smaller standing army than any other nation of her size. Her sons, however, in the face of danger, are ready to leave their desks and their homes to lay down their lives for her. They have shown that our small standing army would thus, in case of war, be augmented by great numbers of voluntary soldiers.

"If the mother country requires the services of her sons," said a colonist of New South Wales, "she could have, not 1000, not 10,000, not 100,000, but the last man we have."

If such patriotism dominates Britons beyond the seas, what of those at home? They will stand by her, as their forefathers have stood, faithful to death. They will fight, not for the object of adding glory to the flag, not to enlarge their possessions, not for the pride of superiority over other nations less fortunate than themselves, but ever to spread freedom and justice for the benefit of the whole world.

With you, then, children of to-day, lies the future of the British Empire. "The old bees die, the young possess the hive," said Shakspere long ages ago.

"Chained to the narrow round of Duty," work on, live on, spend and be spent. Let Nelson's watchword never fail the children of the Empire; let the national ideal never be lowered. Be true to your great trust, true to your home, your country, and your God. And the generation which is passing hence, shall not fear to leave its glorious heritage in the faithful keeping of such as these.

> "O Strength Divine of Roman days,
> O Spirit of the age of Faith,
> Go with our sons on all their ways
> When we long since are dust and wraith."
> —NEWBOLT.

TEACHER'S APPENDIX

Chap.

1. *History of the Thirty Years' Peace.* (1816-1846.) Martineau.

3. *Modern Europe.* Alison Phillips. Vol. viii. (1815-1899.)

   Periods of European History. ed. Hassall.

   Modern Europe. Fyffe. (Abridged, in 1 vol.)

4. *Short History of our Own Times.* M'Carthy.

   Victoria. Fawcett. Eminent Ruler Series.

   The Life of a Century. Hodder. Newnes.

5. *Manual of the History of South Africa.* Wilmot.

   South Africa. Theal. Story of Nations.

   Story of South Africa. Worsfold. Empire Series.

7. *Story of Canada.* Kennedy. Empire Series.

   Canada under British Rule. (1760-1900.) Bourinot. Cambridge Historical Series.

   Short History of our Own Times. M'Carthy.

8. *British America.* British Empire Series.

   Remarkable History of the Hudson's Bay Company. G. Bryce.

9. *The Winning of the West.* Theodore Roosevelt.

   Short History of the United States. M'Carthy.

   America. Doyle. Macmillan's Historical Course.

10. *Sir John Franklin and the North-West Passage.* Markham.

11. *Story of Australia.* F. Shaw. Empire Series.

    Australasia. British Empire Series.

    A History of the Australasian Colonies (to 1893). Jenks. Cambridge Historical Series.

    Australian Commonwealth (to 1890). Story of Nations.

12. *Modern Europe.* Alison Phillips. Vol. viii. (1815-1899.)

    Modern Europe. Fyffe.

    Life of Napoleon III. Arch. Forbes.

13. *Modern Europe.* Fyffe.

Hungary. Vambery. Story of Nations.

14. *Kinglake's Crimea.* (Abridged.)

    Short History of our Own Times. M'Carthy.

15. *Indian Mutiny.* Malleson.

    Rise of the British Dominion in India. Lyall. University Extension Manual.

    Short History of India. T. Wheeler.

    Havelock. Arch. Forbes. English Men of Action.

16. *Makers of Modern Italy.* (Massini, Garibaldi, Cavour.) Marriott.

    Union of Italy. (1815-1893.) Stillman. Cambridge Historical Series.

    Modern Europe. Alison Phillips. Vol. viii.

17. *Ugo Bassi.* (Poem.) Mrs Hamilton King.

18. *United States of America.* (1765-1865.) Channing. Cambridge Historical Series.

    Short History of the United States. M'Carthy.

    Abraham Lincoln and the Downfall of American Slavery. Brooks. Heroes of the Nations.

    Robert Lee and the Southern Confederacy. (1807-1870.) White. Heroes of the

Nations.

Stonewall Jackson and the American Civil War. Henderson.

19. *From Log Cabin to White House.* Thayce.

20. *Modern Europe. Alison Phillips.* Vol. viii.

Germany. (1815-1890.) Headlam. Cambridge Historical Series.

Bismarck and the New German Empire. Headlam. Heroes of the Nations.

21. *Moltke and the Military Supremacy of Germany.* J. Wilkinson. Heroes of the Nations.

Napoleon III. Arch. Forbes.

William I., Emperor of Germany. Arch. Forbes.

22. *Manual of South African History.* Wilmot.

24. *Livingstone.* T. Hughes. English Men of Action.

25. *China.* Douglas. Story of Nations.

26. *Japan.* Murray. Story of Nations.

28. *Russia.* Mortill. Story of Nations.

Expansion of Russia. (1815-1894.) Cambridge Historical Series.

29. *Progress of India, China, and Japan in the Century.* Sir R. Temple. Nineteenth Century Series.

    India, Ceylon, and Straits Settlements. British Empire Series.

20. *Story of Burma.* Story of the Empire Series.

    King Theebaw's Queen. (Fiction.) Fielding.

    Rise of the British Dominion in India. Lyall. University Extension Manual.

31. *Progress of India in the Century.* Temple. Nineteenth Century Series.

32. *Gordon.* Butler. English Men of Action.

    Story of Egypt. Worsfold. Story of Empire Series.

33. *British Africa.* British Empire Series.

    With Kitchener to Khartum. Steevens.

34. *Story of West Africa.* M. Kingsley. Story of Empire Series.

    British Africa. British Empire Series.

35. *Story of Uganda.* Lugard. Story of Empire Series.

    British Africa. British Empire Series.

36. *Manual of South African History.* Wilmot.

37. *Progress of South Africa in the Century.* Theal. Nineteenth Century Series.

38. *Progress of Canada in the Century.* Hopkins. Nineteenth Century Series.

39. *Progress of Australasia in the Century.* Coghlan and Ewing. Nineteenth Century Series.

    Australasia. British Empire Series.

    With the Royal Tour. Knight.

40. *Progress of the United States of America in the Century.* Trent. Nineteenth Century Series.

41. *Progress of the British Empire in the Century.* Stanley Little. Nineteenth Century Series.

    Life of a Century. Hodder. (Popular and Illustrated.)

    Rise of the Empire. Besant. Story of the Empire Series.

42. *Education and Empire.* Haldane.

43. *The Citizen Reader.* Arnold Forster. (Cassells.)

Printed in the United States
135991LV00011B/35/A

9 781599 150178